FIFTY-NINE FAVORITE SONGS

by Franz Schubert

Edited by Eusebius Mandyczewski

From the Breitkopf & Härtel
Complete Works Edition

With new literal prose
translations of the texts

Dover Publications, Inc.
New York

Copyright © 1985 by Dover Publications, Inc.
All rights reserved under Pan American and International Copyright
Conventions.

Published in Canada by General Publishing Company, Ltd., 30 Les-
mill Road, Don Mills, Toronto, Ontario.
Published in the United Kingdom by Constable and Company, Ltd.

This Dover edition, first published in 1985, contains 59 songs selected from *Serie 20. Lieder und Gesänge* (Solo Songs) from *Franz Schubert's
Werke. Kritisch durchgesehene Gesammtausgabe*, originally published by
Breitkopf & Härtel, Leipzig (1884–1897). The new translations of the
texts, the glossary and all other preliminary matter were prepared
specially for the present edition.

Manufactured in the United States of America
Dover Publications, Inc., 31 East 2nd Street, Mineola, N.Y. 11501

Library of Congress Cataloging in Publication Data

Schubert, Franz, 1797–1828.
  [Songs. Selections]
  59 favorite songs.

  Reprint. Selected from: Franz Schubert's Werke. Serie 20, Lieder und
Gesänge. Leipzig: Breitkopf & Härtel, 1884–1897.
  Includes indexes.
  1. Songs with piano.   I. Mandyczewski, Eusebius.
M1620.S38M27   1985   84-759386
ISBN 0-486-24849-6

CONTENTS

The D-numbers are those of the standard thematic catalogue of Schubert's works by Otto Erich Deutsch, in collaboration with Donald R. Wakeling. The present volume follows the order of the Breitkopf & Härtel Complete Works Edition, and that edition's dating of the songs is retained on the respective title pages, but the Deutsch volume should also be consulted on questions of dating and chronological sequence.

GLOSSARY

of German Terms Occurring on the Music Pages

componirt von . . .: composed by . . .
erschienen als . . .: published as . . .
Etwas bewegt(er): somewhat (more) agitatedly
Etwas geschwind(er): somewhat (more) rapidly
Etwas langsam(er): somewhat (more) slowly
Etwas lebhaft: somewhat animatedly
Gedicht von . . .: poem by . . .
Geschwind(er): fast(er)
. . . *gewidmet*: dedicated to . . .
Klarinette: clarinet
lange Haltung: long fermata
Langsam(er): (more) slowly
Langsam, andächtig: slowly, piously
Langsam, feierlich: slowly, solemnly
Langsam, mit aller Kraft: slowly, with full force
Lieblich: sweetly
Mässig: moderately
Mässig geschwind: moderately fast
Mässig, ruhig: moderately, calmly
Mässig, zart: moderately, tenderly
mit erhobener Dämpfung: with damper pedal
mit gehobener Dämpfung: with damper pedal
mit Kraft: with vigor
Mit mehr Bewegung: with more movement

nicht zu geschwind: not too fast
Nicht zu geschwind, doch feurig: not too fast, but
     passionately
nicht zu langsam: not too slowly
Nicht zu schnell, kräftig: not too fast, forcefully
Noch langsamer: still more slowly
Ruhig: calmly
Ruhig und fromm: calmly and piously
Schnell: fast
Sehr langsam: very slowly
sehr leise: very softly
Singstimme: voice
Unruhige Bewegung, doch nicht schnell: with restless
     movement, but not fast
Ursprüngliche Fassung: original version
Vierte Fassung: fourth version
Waldhorn: French horn
Wie anfangs, sehr langsam: as at the beginning, very
     slowly
Wie oben: as above
Ziemlich geschwind: rather fast
Ziemlich langsam: rather slowly
Zweite Bearbeitung (or, Fassung): second version

ALPHABETICAL LIST OF SONG TITLES

ALPHABETICAL LIST OF SONG OPENINGS

ALPHABETICAL LIST
OF POETS

TRANSLATIONS

Poets' last names appear in parentheses; for full names and dates, see Alphabetical List of Poets, p. vii. Even for the German texts translated from English poets, a literal translation from the German is provided here.

Des Mädchens Klage/The Girl's Lament
(Schiller)

The oak wood rages, the clouds go by, the girl sits on the green shore; the waves break forcefully, forcefully, and she sends sighs into the dark night, her eyes dimmed with weeping.

"My heart has died, the world is empty and will no longer give me anything I wish for. Holy Maid, call back your child; I have tasted earthly happiness, I have lived and loved."

"Your tears trickle down in vain, lamenting does not awaken the dead; but tell me what will comfort and heal your heart, after sweet love's pleasure has disappeared; I in heaven will not refuse it."

"Let my tears trickle down in vain, what if lamenting does not awaken the dead! The sweetest happiness for the mourning heart, after beautiful love's pleasure has disappeared, is love's sorrows and laments."

Hoffnung/Hope
(Schiller)

People talk and dream a great deal about better days in the future; they can be seen running and chasing after a fortunate, golden object. The world grows old and becomes young again, but man always hopes for improvement, but man always hopes for improvement.

Hope introduces him to life, it hovers about the happy child; its magic glow lures the youth, and it is not buried with the old man; for even when he ends his weary course in the grave, he still raises a banner to hope at his grave.

It is no empty, flattering delusion, generated in the brain of a fool. Our heart announces it loudly: we are born for something better; and what our inner voice says, does not deceive the soul that hopes.

An den Frühling/To Spring
(Schiller)

Welcome, fair youth, nature's bliss! With your basket of flowers, welcome to the meadow, welcome to the meadow! Ah! Ah! Here you are again! And you are so lovely and beautiful! And we are so sincerely happy to go out to meet you, to go out to meet you.

And are you still thinking about the girl I love? Ah, my friend, do think about her! There my girl loved me, and the girl still loves me, and the girl still loves me! You gave me many a flower for my girl at my request; I come and ask again, and you? You will give them to me. And you? You will give them to me.

Dem Unendlichen/To the Infinite
(Klopstock)

How my heart soars when it thinks about you, infinite one! How it sinks when it looks down upon itself! Then, lamenting, it beholds misery, and night and death! But you summon me out of my night, you who help in misery, in death! Then I know fully that you created me eternally, splendid one, for whom no song of praise, at the grave below, at the throne above—Lord God—for whom no song of jubilation, ablaze with gratitude, is sufficient! Rustle, trees of life, to the tones of the harp! Babble along with them to the tones of the harp, crystal stream! Your murmuring and babbling, and your tones, o harps, can never express it completely: it is God, it is God that you praise. Worlds, thunder in your solemn course! Worlds, thunder in the trombone choir! Resound, all you suns, on the road full of light, in the trombone choir! You worlds, you thunder, you, the trombone choir, can never sound it completely—God, never completely—it is God, God, God that you praise!

An den Mond/To the Moon
(Hölty)

Why do you peep so brightly and clearly through these apple trees where your friend was once so happy and dreamt sweet dreams? Cloak your silvery light and merely glimmer, as you glimmer when you glitter upon the premature funeral wreath of a young bride!

It is in vain that you look down so brightly and clearly into this arbor; you will never again find the happy pair in its shade! A dark, hostile fate snatched my beautiful girl from me! No sigh can conjure her back, and no tear of longing!

Oh, if she ever happens to walk by my resting place, then suddenly make the flowers on my grave bright with a dim beam! Let her sit down on the grave, weeping, where roses hang down, and let her pick a flower and press it to her cheek.

Der Wanderer/The Traveler
(Schmidt von Lübeck)

I arrive from the mountains; the valley is steamy with mist, the sea roars, the sea roars. I walk in silence, am seldom happy, and my sighs always ask "Where?," always ask "Where?" The sun here seems so cold to me, the blossoms seem withered, life seems old, and what people say seems empty noise—I am a stranger everywhere. Where are you, where are you, country that I love? I seek for you, I have premonitions of you, but I never know you. That land, that land so green with hope, so green with hope, that land where my roses bloom, where my friends walk up and down, where my departed ones come back to life, the land that speaks my language—O land, where are you? I walk in silence, am seldom happy, and my sighs always ask "Where?," always ask "Where?" In a ghostly breath, the echo replies to me: "Where you are not, there happiness is."

Lied eines Schiffers an die Dioskuren
Song of a Seaman to the Dioscuri
(Mayrhofer)

Dioscuri, twin stars lighting my ship's way, I am set at ease on the sea by your gentleness, by your wakefulness, by your gentleness, by your wakefulness. Even the man who has firm self-confidence and faces the storm without flinching, still feels doubly courageous and blessed in your rays. This oar that I ply to sunder the waves of the sea, I will hang upon the columns of your temple when I return safely, Dioscuri, twin stars!

Wiegenlied/Lullaby
(Claudius?)

Sleep, sleep, lovely, sweet boy; your mother's hand rocks you gently; this cradle's swinging brings you quiet rest, gentle balm.

Sleep, sleep in your sweet grave; your mother's arm still protects you; in her love she embraces all your wishes, all your belongings, all of them warm with love.

Sleep, sleep in the bosom of your bed of down; a loud note of love still sounds around you; a lily or a rose, when you awake you will have it as a reward.

Abendlied/Evening Song
(Claudius)

The moon has risen, the little golden stars gleam in the sky brightly and clearly; the forest stands dark and silent, and from the pastures white mist rises wondrously.

How quiet the world is, and so intimate and lovely in its cloak of twilight!—like a quiet chamber in which you are to sleep and forget the day's sorrow.

Do you see the moon there? It is only half visible and yet it is round and beautiful! Probably many things are like that, things that we readily laugh at because our eyes don't see them.

We proud sons of man are nothing but poor sinners, and don't know much. We build castles in the air and seek out many arts and get further from our goal.

God, let us see Your salvation, let us not trust in perishable things or take pleasure in vanity! Let us become simple and stand before You here on earth pious and happy as children.

Der Tod und das Mädchen/Death and the Maiden
(Claudius)

[The girl:] "Go away, oh, go away, you fierce skeleton! I am still young; go, my friend, and don't touch me, and don't touch me."

[Death:] "Give me your hand, you beautiful, delicate creature; I am a friend and do not come to punish. Be of good cheer! I am not fierce; you shall sleep softly in my arms."

An die Musik/To Music
(Schober)

You lovely art, in how many gray hours when I was ensnared in life's fierce circle, have you sparked my heart to warm love, whisked me away to a better world, away to a better world!

Often a sigh escaping from your harp, one of your sweet, holy chords, has revealed to me a heaven of better times; you lovely art, I thank you for that, you lovely art, I thank you.

Die Forelle/The Trout
(Schubart)

In a bright brook the capricious trout shot by like an arrow in its happy haste. I stood on the bank and in sweet repose watched the merry fish swimming in the clear brook, the merry fish swimming in the clear brook.

A fisherman with his rod stood on the bank and cold-bloodedly watched the fish darting about. I thought, "As long as the water does not lack clarity, he will never catch the trout with his line, he will never catch the trout with his line."

But finally the thief lost patience; he slyly muddied the brook, and before I knew it his rod twitched and the little fish, the little fish was wriggling on the hook. And I, all excited, looked at the deceived victim, and I, all excited, looked at the deceived victim.

Gruppe aus dem Tartarus / Group in Tartarus
(Schiller)

Listen—like the muttering of the enraged sea, as a brook sobs through a basin of hollow rocks, over there, muffled and deep, a heavy, empty "Ah!" is groaned forth, exacted by suffering. Pain distorts their faces; despair opens wide their maw in a curse. Their eyes are hollow; their glances fearfully seek out the bridge over Cocytus, and, with tears, follow its mournful course, its mournful course. They ask one another in anxious low tones whether their time is not yet up. They ask one another in anxious low tones whether their time is not yet up, whether their time is not yet up, whether their time is not yet up. Eternity, eternity circles above them and breaks Saturn's scythe in two. Eternity circles above them and breaks Saturn's scythe in two, and breaks Saturn's scythe in two.

Der Alpenjäger / The Alpine Hunter
(Schiller)

"Don't you want to guard the lamb? The lamb is so well-behaved and gentle, feeds upon grass blossoms, playing by the edge of the brook." "Mother, mother, let me go hunting on the mountain heights, hunting on the mountain heights!"

"Don't you want to call the flock with the merry sound of the horn? The tinkling of their bells harmonizes beautifully with the happy song of the forest." "Mother, mother, let me go roaming on the wild heights, roaming on the wild heights!"

"Don't you want to tend the flowers that grow so friendly in the flowerbed? Out there no garden invites you, it is wild on the wild heights!" "Let the flowers bloom, mother, mother, let me leave, mother, mother, let me leave!"

And the boy went hunting; his emotions drive and tear him away, off without delay in his blind daring to the dark places on the mountain; the trembling chamois flees before him with the speed of the wind.

It climbs with airy energy onto the naked ribs of the rocks, its bold leap carries it through the gap in the split cliffs; but daringly he follows it with his deadly bow.

Now it teeters on the rough pinnacles, on the highest ridge, where the rocks plunge precipitously and the path has vanished; below it is the steep height, behind it is the nearness of the enemy.

With the mute glances of sorrow it begs the cruel man, begs in vain, for he is already bending his bow and ready to shoot. Suddenly from the rift in the rocks steps the spirit, the old man of the mountain. And with his divine hands he protects the tortured animal. "Must you send death and sorrow," he calls, "even up here where I dwell? The earth has room for all; why are you persecuting my flock, why are you persecuting my flock?"

Litaney auf das Fest Aller Seelen / Litany for All Souls' Day
(Jacobi)

They rest in peace, all the souls that have terminated a fearful sorrow or have ended a sweet dream, sated with life or scarcely born, departed from the world: all souls rest in peace!

Those who sought comrades here, more often wept, never cursed when no one ever understood the grasp of their faithful hands: all who have departed from here, all souls rest in peace!

The souls of lovely girls, whose tears cannot be counted, who were abandoned by a false lover and rejected by the blind world: all who have departed from here, all souls rest in peace!

And the youth to whose grave, secretly, early in the morning, his bride brings a taper, because love laid him in his grave: all who have departed from here, all souls rest in peace!

All the spirits who, full of clarity, became martyrs to the truth, fought for the shrine, did not seek martyrs' glory: all who have departed from here, all souls rest in peace!

And those who never laughed with the sun, but lay awake on thorns beneath the moon, in order to see God face to face in the future in the pure light of Heaven: all who have departed from here, all souls rest in peace!

And those who liked to linger by the joyous wine cup in a rose garden but then, when times were bad, tasted the cup's bitterness: all those who have departed from here, all souls rest in peace!

Also those who knew no peace but sent their courage and strength over a corpse-strewn field into the half-slumbering world: all those who have departed from here, all souls rest in peace!

They rest in peace, all the souls that have terminated a fearful sorrow or have ended a sweet dream, sated with life or scarcely born, departed from the world: all souls rest in peace!

Der Wanderer / The Traveler
(F. v. Schlegel)

How clearly the moonlight speaks to me, encouraging me to travel: "Follow the old track faithfully, choose no dwelling place. Or else heavy days will bring eternal sorrow. You must wander forth to see others, you must travel, easily escaping all laments." With a gentle ebb and a high tide deep in my mind, I travel farther thus in the dark, climb courageously, sing merrily, and the world looks good to me. I see all pure things in a soft reflection, I see nothing tangled and dried up in the day's heat: happy in my surroundings, but alone.

Das Mädchen / The Girl
(F. v. Schlegel)

How deeply, I would say, my lover devotes himself to me, in order to relieve my sad realization that he does not love so deeply. When I want to say it, it escapes; if I had the gift of musical tones, it would float away in harmonies, for it lives in that music. Only the nightingale can say how deeply he devotes himself to me, in order to relieve my sad realization that he does not love so deeply.

Sehnsucht / Longing
(Schiller)

Ah, if I could find the way out of this low valley, on which the cold mist lies heavily, ah, how happy I would feel, ah, how happy I would feel! Over there I espy beautiful hills, eternally young and eternally green! If I had pinions, if I had wings, I would fly to the hills, I would fly to the hills. I hear harmonies sounding, notes of sweet heavenly peace; and the light winds waft healing fragrance my way. I see golden fruit glowing, beckoning from the dark foliage, beckoning from the dark foliage, and the flowers that bloom there are not despoiled by any winter, are not despoiled by any winter. Oh, how beautiful life must be there in the everlasting sunshine! And the air on those heights, oh, how refreshing it must be! But I am hindered by the raging of the river that furiously roars between; its waves are rising so high that my soul shudders. I see a boat tossing, but ah! the boatman is missing! Board it quickly and without delay! Its sails are stirring, its sails are stirring; board it quickly and without delay! You must have faith, you must have courage, for the gods are no pawnbrokers; only a miracle can carry you to the beautiful land of miracles. You must have faith, you must have courage, for the gods are no pawnbrokers; only a miracle can carry you to the beautiful land of miracles, to the beautiful land of miracles.

Der Jüngling am Bache/The Boy by the Brook
(Schiller)

By the spring the boy sat; he made himself a wreath of flowers, he made himself a wreath of flowers, and he saw it swept away and drifting on the dancing waves, drifting on the dancing waves. And thus my days flee by, unresting as the brook! And so my youth fades, as wreaths soon wither, as wreaths soon wither!

Do not ask why I am mournful at my vigorous time of life, at my vigorous time of life! Everyone is happy and hopeful when springtime is renewed, when springtime is renewed. But these thousand voices of awakening nature arouse only heavy anguish deep within my breast, only heavy anguish.

What am I to do with the joy that beautiful springtime offers me? There is only one woman whom I seek; she is near and infinitely far. Lovingly I reach out to grasp the beloved shadow; alas, I cannot attain it, and my heart remains unsatisfied.

Come down, you beautiful dear one, and leave your proud castle! I shall strew in your lap flowers that the spring has borne. Listen—the grove resounds with song and the brook murmurs brightly! There is room in the smallest hut for a happy loving couple.

Nachtstück/Nocturne
(Mayrhofer)

When the mist spreads over mountains and Luna battles against clouds, the old man takes his harp, walks into the woods and sings in low tones: "You holy night! Soon it shall be over. Soon I shall sleep the long slumber that will release me from all sorrow, that will release me from all sorrow. You holy night! Soon it shall be over. Soon I shall sleep the long slumber that will release me from all sorrow, that will release me from all sorrow. Then the green trees will rustle: "Sleep sweetly, you good old man." The grasses will continually whisper as they wave: "We cover his resting place." Then the green trees will rustle: "Sleep sweetly, you good old man." And many a dear bird will call: "Oh, let him rest in his tomb of sod, oh, let him rest in his tomb of sod!" The old man listens, the old man is silent. Death has bent over him, Death has bent over him.

Die Vögel/The Birds
(F. v. Schlegel)

How lovely and jolly, to soar, to sing, to look down upon the earth from gleaming heights! People are foolish, they can't fly, they can't fly. They lament in their suffering, we flutter toward heaven, we flutter toward heaven. The hunter wants to kill us because we pecked at his fruit; we must deride him and win booty.

Frühlingsglaube/Springtime Credo
(Uhland)

The gentle breezes have awakened, they murmur and weave in and out day and night, they are busy everywhere, everywhere. Oh, fresh fragrance, oh, new melody! Oh, new melody! Now, my poor heart, don't be fearful; now everything, everything must take a new turn, now everything, everything must take a new turn. The world grows more beautiful every day; you can't tell what may yet develop; there is no end to the blossoming, there is no end to it. The furthest, deepest valley is blooming, the deepest valley is blooming; now, my poor heart, forget your sorrow; now everything, everything must take a new turn, now everything, everything must take a new turn.

Der Jüngling an der Quelle/The Boy by the Fountain
(Salis)

Be quiet, rippling spring and you waving, whispering poplars; your slumber-sound only reawakens my love. I sought relief near you, trying to forget her, the obstinate girl. Oh, but leaves and brook are sighing "Luise" to me; oh, but leaves and brook are sighing "Luise" to me. Luise! Luise!

Sei mir gegrüsst!/I Greet You!
(Rückert)

Oh, woman snatched away from me and my kisses, I greet you, I kiss you, I kiss you! Though you are attainable only by a greeting born of my longing, I greet you, I kiss you, I kiss you! You that were given to my heart by the hand of Love! You who were taken away from my bosom! With this outpouring of tears I greet you, I kiss you, I kiss you! In spite of the distance that has placed itself between you and me, separating us in hostile fashion; in despite of the envy of the powers of fate, I greet you, I kiss you, I kiss you! As you once in the loveliest springtime of love came to meet me with greetings and kisses, with the most ardent outpouring of my soul I greet you, I kiss you, I kiss you! One breath of love annihilates space and time; I am with you, you are with me, I hold you in my arm's embrace, I greet you, I kiss you, I kiss you!

Nachtviolen/Dameworts [literally, Night Violets]
(Mayrhofer)

Night violets! Night violets! Dark eyes full of soul, it is bliss to be immersed in that velvety blue, in that velvety blue. Green leaves reach out happily to brighten you, to adorn you; but you gaze seriously and silently into the warm spring air. You have struck my loyal heart with lofty beams of melancholy, and now our sacred alliance continues to blossom through the wordless nights, now our sacred alliance continues to blossom through the wordless nights.

Selige Welt/Blissful World
(Senn)

I drift upon the sea of life, I sit at ease in my boat; no destination and no steering, here and there as the current draws, as the winds blow. The deluded seek one blissful island, the deluded seek one blissful island, but there is not just one, but there is not just one. Put to land anywhere with confidence, anywhere that the sea breaks upon the soil.

Schwanengesang/Swan Song
(Senn)

"How can I fully lament the feeling of death that paralyzingly races through my limbs? How can I fully sing of the feeling of transformation that liberatingly wafts over you, my spirit?" He lamented, he sang in the fear of annihilation, in the joy of transfiguration, until life departed. That is the meaning of the swan's song.

An die Leyer/To the Lyre
(Bruchmann, after Anacreon)

I want to sing of the sons of Atreus, or about Cadmus! But my strings resound only with love ringing out, but my strings resound only with love ringing out. I changed the strings; I would like to exchange the lyre; the victorious exploits of Hercules shall sound forth from its power! But these strings too resound only with love ringing out, but these strings too resound only with love ringing out. Farewell, then, heroes, for my strings, instead of threatening with heroic song, resound only with love ringing out. Farewell, then, heroes, for my strings, instead of threatening with heroic song, resound only with love ringing out.

Der Zwerg/The Dwarf
(Collin)

The mountains are already disappearing in the dim light, the ship glides over smooth ocean waves; on it are the queen with her dwarf. She looks up toward the high-vaulted arch of the sky, up toward the far blue regions embroidered with light and laced with the pale milk of heaven. "Never, never yet have you lied to me, you stars!" Thus she exclaims. "Now I shall soon disappear—you are telling me so—but I am truly glad to die." Then the dwarf walks toward the queen; he would like to tie the ribbon of red silk around her neck; he weeps and weeps as if he wished to become quickly blind with grief, blind with grief. He speaks: "You yourself are to blame for this sorrow, because you abandoned me for the king; now your death arouses only joy in me, only joy in me. Of course I will eternally hate myself for having killed you with my own hands, but now you must grow pale in premature death." She places her hand upon her heart so full of young life, and heavy tears flow from her eyes as she tries to raise them to heaven in prayer. "May you not gain sorrow through my death!" she says. Then the dwarf kisses her pale cheeks, and immediately she loses consciousness. The dwarf looks at the woman lying in the grip of death; he lowers her deep into the sea with his own hands. His heart yearns for her with such great desire, his heart yearns for her with such great desire, with such great desire. He will never again land on any coast.

Wehmuth/Melancholy
(Collin)

When I walk through forest and fields, my restless heart feels so good but so sad at the same time; so good, so sad, when I see the meadow at the height of its beauty and all the pleasure of springtime. Because all that blows in the rustling wind, all that towers up toward heaven, and man as well, who feels so much at home with all the beauty that he sees, disappears and perishes, disappears and perishes, and perishes.

Auf dem Wasser zu singen/Boating Song
(Stolberg)

Amid the glitter of the playful waves the rocking boat glides like swans; ah, on the softly glittering waves of joy the soul glides away like the boat; ah, on the softly glittering waves of joy the soul glides away like the boat; for pouring down from heaven onto the waves, sunset dances around the boat, sunset dances around the boat.

Above the treetops of the western grove the reddish glow beckons us in friendly fashion; under the branches of the eastern grove the sweet flag rustles in the reddish glow; under the branches of the eastern grove the sweet flag rustles in the reddish glow; the joy of heaven and the repose of the grove are breathed in by the soul in the reddening glow, are breathed in by the soul in the reddening glow.

Ah, time escapes me with dewy wing on the cradling waves; let time escape again tomorrow with glittering wing as it did yesterday and today; let time escape again tomorrow with glittering wing as it did yesterday and today, until with loftier, radiant wings I myself escape from changeable time, I myself escape from changeable time.

Der Pilgrim/The Pilgrim
(Schiller)

I was still in the springtime of my life when I set off on my travels, leaving the happy dances of youth behind in my father's house. I threw away all my inheritance and belongings in happy self-confidence, and leaning on my light pilgrim's staff I set out with a childlike mind. For I was urged onward by a mighty hope and an obscure message of faith. "Travel," it called, "the road is clear, keep moving on to higher ground—until you reach a golden portal; then go in, for earthly things will be heavenly and imperishable there." It became evening and it became morning; never, never did I linger in one place, but what I seek, what I want, has always remained hidden. Mountains lay in the way, rivers obstructed my progress; I built paths over precipices, bridges across raging torrents. And I came to the banks of a river that flowed eastward; joyfully trusting in its guidance, I plunged into its bosom. The play of its waves bore me out to a great sea, which lies before me in an empty expanse, it lies before me in an empty expanse; I am no closer to my goal, I am no closer to my goal. Alas, no road will lead there; alas, the sky above me will never touch the earth, and "there" is never here, is never here, and "there" is never here, is never here!

Dass sie hier gewesen/That They Were Here
(Rückert)

The east wind's breathing fragrance into the breeze is its way of announcing that you were here, that you were here. Tears flowing here inform you, if you had no other way of knowing, that I was here, that I was here. Beauty and love—could they remain concealed? Fragrance and tears make it known that they were here, that they were here; fragrance and tears make it known that they were here, that they were here.

Du bist die Ruh/You Are Repose
(Rückert)

You are repose, gentle peace; you are longing and that which satisfies longing. Full of pleasure and pain, I consecrate to you as a dwelling here my eyes and heart, my eyes and heart. Come into my abode and close the door quietly behind you. Drive other sorrow out of my breast! May my heart be filled with the pleasure of you, with the pleasure of you. The tabernacle of my eyes, illuminated by your radiance alone—oh, fill it completely, oh, fill it completely. The tabernacle of my eyes, illuminated by your radiance alone—oh, fill it completely, oh, fill it completely.

Lachen und Weinen/Laughing and Weeping
(Rückert)

With love there are so many reasons for laughing and weeping all the time. In the morning I laughed with joy; and why I now weep in the glow of evening, I myself cannot tell, I myself cannot tell. With love there are so many reasons for laughing and weeping all the time. In the evening I wept with pain; and why you can wake up laughing in the morning—that I must ask you, my heart, that I must ask you, my heart.

Im Abendroth/In the Sunset
(Lappe)

Oh, how beautiful is Your world, Father, when it has a golden radiance, when Your glow pours down and paints the dust with shimmering light; when the red that flashes in the clouds sinks into my silent window. Could I lament? Could I be fearful? Lack faith in You and myself? No, I shall bear Your heaven in my bosom while still on earth, and my heart,

before it stops beating, will still drink in brightness and still quaff light.

Der Einsame/The Solitary Man
(Lappe)

When my crickets chirp at night by the hearth that has warmed up late, I sit down with contented mind cozily by the fire, I sit down with contented mind cozily by the fire, so carefree, so unburdened, so carefree, so unburdened. It is a pleasure to stay awake by the fire for another intimate, quiet hour; you poke up the sparks when the flame gets low, and you meditate and think: another day gone by, another day gone by! Whatever pleasure or pain its course has brought for us, whatever pleasure or pain its course has brought for us, passes once more through our mind; but we reject the unpleasant so it doesn't disturb our night, so it doesn't disturb our night. Comfortably you prepare yourself for a happy dream; when, free from worries, a lovely image fills the soul with gentle pleasure, one goes to bed, one goes to bed. Oh, how I enjoy my quiet country life! The things that enchained my confused heart in the swarming, loud world, give no contentment, give no contentment. Keep chirping, dear crickets, in my hermitage, narrow and small; keep chirping, dear crickets, in my hermitage, narrow and small; I like to have you here, you don't annoy me. When your song breaks the silence, I am not altogether alone, I am not altogether alone; when your song breaks the silence, I am not altogether alone, I am not altogether alone, I am not altogether alone.

Todtengräbers Heimwehe
The Gravedigger's Homesickness
(Craigher)

O humanity, o life, what does it mean, oh, what does it mean? Dig the hole, cover it up, no repose day or night! The pressure, the urgency, to what end, oh, to what end? "To the grave, deep down to the grave!" O fate, o sad duty, I can't bear it any more! When will you sound, o hour of rest? O Death, come and close my eyes, come and close my eyes! Life is oh, so hot and oppressive, oh, so hot and oppressive; the grave is so peaceful, so cool! But, alas! Who will lay me in it? I am here alone, so all alone, so all alone! Who will lay me in it, who will lay me in it? Abandoned by all, related only to death, I linger on the edge, the cross in my hand, and stare with longing gaze down into the deep, deep grave! O home of peace, land of the blessed, my soul is tied to you by a magical bond! You beckon to me from afar, you eternal light; you beckon to me from afar, you eternal light! The stars disappear, my eyes are already glazing over; the stars disappear, my eyes are already glazing over! I sink, I sink! Beloved ones, I am coming; beloved ones, I am coming! I sink, I sink! Beloved ones, I am coming; beloved ones, I am coming! I am coming, I am coming! I am coming, I am coming!

Die junge Nonne/The Young Nun
(Craigher)

How the howling storm roars through the treetops! The beams groan, the house trembles! The thunder rolls, the lightning flashes! And the night is dark, the night is dark as the grave! Go right on, go right on! That's the way the storm still raged in me, too, recently! Life roared as the storm does now! My limbs quivered as the house does now! Love flamed as the lightning does now! And my heart was dark, my heart was dark as the grave! Now rage, you wild, mighty storm! In my heart is peace, in my heart is repose! The loving bride awaits the Bridegroom; purified in the ordeal of fire, she is wedded to eternal, eternal Love. I wait, my Savior, with longing gaze. Come, heavenly Bridegroom, fetch Your bride! Release my soul from its earthly bondage! Listen! Peacefully rings the bell from the tower; the sweet sound lures me almightily to eternal heights; the sweet sound lures me almightily to eternal heights: hallelujah, hallelujah!

Nacht und Träume/Night and Dreams
(Collin)

Sacred night, you descend; dreams, also, flow down—as your moonlight does through space—through people's quiet, quiet hearts. They listen to them with pleasure, they listen to them with pleasure, and call when the day awakens: "Return, lovely night! Lovely dreams, return; lovely dreams, return!"

Ellen's Gesang. III. Hymne an die Jungfrau.
Aus Walter Scott's "Fräulein vom See"
Ellen's Song (3): Hymn to the Virgin ["Ave Maria"],
from Scott's *Lady of the Lake*
(Storck)

Ave Maria! Gentle Virgin! Grant a virgin's prayer! From this crag, stiff and wild, my prayer shall be wafted up to you. We sleep in security till the morning even though people are so cruel. O Virgin, see the virgin's sorrows; o Mother, hear a child's request! Ave Maria!

Ave Maria! Spotless one! When we fall asleep on this crag and your protection covers us, the hard rock will seem soft to us. You smile and the fragrance of roses is wafted through this damp, rocky grave. O Mother, hear a child's entreaty; o Virgin, a virgin calls! Ave Maria!

Ave Maria! Pure maid! The demons of earth and sky, driven off by the grace of your eyes, cannot dwell with us here! We will quietly submit to fate since your holy solace descends upon us. Graciously stoop down to the virgin, to the child who prays for her father! Ave Maria!

Auf der Bruck
At the Bruck [excursion locality near Göttingen]
(Schulze)

Trot gaily without repose, my good steed, through night and rain! Why do you fear bushes and boughs and stumble on the wild paths? Even though the forest stretches deep and densely, it must still finally open up again, and in friendly fashion a distant light, and in friendly fashion a distant light will greet us from the dark valley. I wish I could fly on your slender back over mountains and fields, and take pleasure in the variegated ways of the world and in lovely views. Many glances smile at me intimately and offer me peace, love and joy, and yet I hasten on without resting, and yet I hasten on

without resting and return, return to my sorrow. For it is three days now that I have been far from the woman who has bound me forever; for three days sun, stars, earth and sky had vanished for me. Of the pleasure and sorrows that in her company now soothed my heart and now tore it apart, for three days I felt only the pain and, alas! had to do without the joy, and, alas! had to do without the joy. Far over land and lake we see the birds flying to warmer fields; how then should love ever mistake its road? So then, trot courageously through the night! And even if the dark paths disappear, the clear eyes of longing stay awake, the clear eyes of longing stay awake, and I am led unmistakably onward by a sweet premonition; the clear eyes of longing stay awake, the clear eyes of longing stay awake, and I am led unmistakably onward by a sweet premonition.

Das Heimweh/Homesickness
(Pyrker)

Ah, the son of the mountains is devoted to his homeland with childlike love, is devoted to his homeland with childlike love. Just as the flower stolen from the Alps withers away, so he withers away when torn from his home; just as the flower stolen from the Alps withers away, so he withers away when torn from his home, when torn away he withers. Constantly he sees the familiar cottage in which he was born as it stands amid the bright green of the fragrance-spreading alpine meadows; constantly he sees the familiar cottage in which he was born as it stands amid the bright green of the fragrance-spreading alpine meadows. He sees the dark pine copse, the mountainside towering over it, and mountain beyond mountain piled up in awesome majesty and glowing in the pink light of evening, and glowing in the pink light of evening. The vision is always before him, the vision is always before him; ah, the familiar cottage, in the pink light of evening— the vision is always before him. Everything around him is darkened, everything around him is darkened. Anxiously he listens; he thinks he hears the lowing of the cows from the nearby strip of woods, and cowbells ringing down from high up in the Alps. He thinks he hears the call of the cowherds or a song of the dairymaid, who with an intermittent call merrily pours forth alpine melodies that echo back to her. He always hears the sound following him, he always hears the sound following him. He is not charmed by the grace of the smiling plains; in solitude he shuns the encompassing walls of cities and, breaking into tears, he views from a hilltop his native mountains. Ah, irresistible longing draws him there, draws him there; ah, irresistible longing draws him there, draws him there; breaking into tears, he views from a hilltop his native mountains, from the hill, in tears, his native mountains; ah, irresistible longing draws him there, draws him there; ah, irresistible longing, irresistible longing draws him there, draws him there.

Die Allmacht/The Almighty
(Pyrker)

Great is Jehovah the Lord, far heaven and earth declare His power; great is Jehovah the Lord, far heaven and earth declare His power. You can hear it in the roar of the storm, in the loudly raging call of the woodland torrent; great is Jehovah the Lord; you can hear it in the roar of the storm, in the loudly raging call of the woodland torrent; great is Jehovah the Lord; great is His power. You can hear it in the murmur of the forest growing green, you can see it in the gold of the waving grain, in the glowing colors of lovely flowers, in the shining of the star-sown sky, in the shining of the star-sown sky, in the glowing colors of lovely flowers, in the shining of the star-sown sky, in the shining of the star-sown sky. Fearfully it rumbles in the drumroll of the thunder and flames in the lightning's swift, jagged flight; but your pounding heart announces to you even more tangibly the power of Jehovah, but your pounding heart announces to you even more tangibly the power of Jehovah, the everlasting God, when you look upward beseechingly and hope for grace and mercy, when you look upward beseechingly and hope for grace and mercy. Great is Jehovah the Lord, great is Jehovah the Lord.

Sehnsucht/Longing
(Seidl)

The pane freezes, the wind is rough, the night sky clear and blue. I sit in my little room and gaze into the clear blue, and gaze into the clear blue. I lack something, I feel it all too well, I am without my sweetheart, that faithful person; and when I want to look at the stars, tears always flow from my eyes, tears always flow from my eyes. My love, where are you lingering so far away, my beautiful star, apple of my eye? You know I really love you and need you, I really love you and need you; again I am close to tears. So I have tortured myself so many days because none of my songs will come out right; they can't be pinned down but they whistle away like the west wind, but they whistle away like the west wind. What a gentle warmth has just come over me again! Look, that has turned into a song! When my fate has separated me from my sweetheart, then I feel that I am permitted to sing, then I feel that I am permitted to sing, that I am permitted to sing.

Fischerweise/Fisherman's Tune
(Schlechta)

The fisherman is not assailed by worries, sorrow or pain. He unties his boat early in the morning with a light heart, with a light heart. At that time peace still lies all about on forest, field and brook; he awakens the golden sun with his song, he awakens the golden sun with his song. At that time peace still lies all about on forest, field and brook; he awakens the golden sun with his song.

He sings as he works with a full, fresh voice; his labors give him strength, strength gives him pleasure in life, strength gives him pleasure in life. Soon a colorful school of fish can be heard down in the depths, splashing through the sky reflected in the water, splashing through the sky reflected in the water. Soon a colorful school of fish can be heard down in the depths, splashing through the sky reflected in the water. But the man who wants to cast a net needs clear, good eyes; he must be merry as the waves and free as the current; he must be merry as the waves and free as the current. There on the bridge the shepherdess is fishing with a rod—the sly minx! Give up your cunning, give up your cunning, *that* fish you won't deceive. There on the bridge the shepherdess is fishing with a rod—the sly minx! Give up your cunning, that fish you won't deceive.

Im Frühling/In the Spring
(Schulze)

I sit quietly on the slope of the hill; the sky is so clear; the breeze plays in the green valley where at the first day of spring I was once oh, so happy, so happy—where I walked by her side so familiarly and so closely, and saw the beautiful sky blue and bright deep down in the dark, rocky fountain; and saw her in the sky, and saw her in the sky. See how colorful springtime already peeps from buds and blossoms. Not all blossoms are the same to me; I would most like to pick one from the branch from which she picked, from which she picked. For everything is still as it was then, the flowers, the open country; the sun shines no less brightly; no less friendly is the blue image of the sky floating in the fountain, the blue image of the sky. Only the will and delusion change, only pleasure and hostility change places; the happiness of love flies away, and only love remains behind, love and alas! sorrow, and alas! sorrow. Oh, if I were only a little bird there on the hillside meadow, then I would stay on the branches here and sing a sweet song about her all summer long, all summer long; I would sing about her all summer long.

Über Wildemann, einem Bergstädtchen am Harz
Above Wildemann, a Town in the Harz Mountains
(Schulze)

The winds roar on the fir-clad mountainside; the streams rush down the valley; I walk hastily through forest and snow, many a mile from height to height; I walk hastily through forest and snow, many a mile from height to height, from height to height. And even if life in the open valley already strives to raise itself into the sunlight, I must pass by with a stormy mind and I prefer to look toward the winter. On green heaths, on colorful meadows, I would always have to see only my sorrow: that even on stones life puts forth shoots, and, alas! only one woman seals her heart shut, only one woman seals her heart shut. O love, love, o breath of May! You force the buds out of trees and bushes! The birds sing on green heights, fountains spring up as you waft by, fountains spring up as you waft by! You let me roam, filled with dark delusion, through the screaming of the wind on a rugged path. O glittering of spring, o glow of blossoms, shall I then never enjoy you? O glittering of spring, o glow of blossoms, shall I then never enjoy you, never enjoy you?

Ständchen aus Shakespeare's "Cymbelin"
Serenade from Shakespeare's *Cymbeline*
["Hark, Hark! the Lark"]
(A. W. v Schlegel)

Hark, hark! the lark in the blue of the sky; and Phoebus, newly awakened, waters his steeds with the dew that covers flower calyxes, that covers flower calyxes. The bud of the marigold opens its little golden eyes; along with everything that is called charming, get up, you sweet maiden; along with everything that is called charming, get up, you sweet maiden, get up, get up, you sweet maiden, get up, get up, get up, you sweet maiden, get up!

Gesang (An Sylvia)
aus Shakespeare's "Die beiden Edelleute von Verona"
Song (To Sylvia) ["Who Is Sylvia"]
from Shakespeare's *Two Gentlemen of Verona*
(Bauernfeld)

What is Sylvia, tell me, that the broad meadow praises her? I see her approach beautiful and gentle; it points to the favor and the mark of heaven that everything submits to her, that everything submits to her.

Is she beautiful and kind as well? Charm soothes like gentle childhood. Amor hastens toward her eyes; there he cures his blindness and lingers in sweet repose, and lingers in sweet repose.

Therefore, my song, sing of Sylvia; praise be to lovely Sylvia! She surpasses by far every attraction that earth can grant: garlands for her and music of strings, garlands for her and music of strings!

Der Wanderer an den Mond
The Traveler's Address to the Moon
(Seidl)

I on the earth, you in the sky, we both travel briskly: I serious and melancholy, you gentle and pure—what causes the difference? I travel as a stranger from land to land, so homeless, so unknown, up the mountains, down the mountains, into the forests, out of the forests, but nowhere, alas! am I at home. But you travel up and down, from your cradle in the east to your grave in the west; you rove in and out of different countries and yet, wherever you are, you are at home! The sky, in its infinite expanse, is your beloved homeland. How happy is the man who, wherever he goes, is still standing on his native soil; how happy is the man who, wherever he goes, is still standing on his native soil, standing on his native soil!

Bei dir allein
Only with You [No. II of *Vier Refrain-Lieder*]
(Seidl)

Only with you do I feel that I am alive, that I am filled with youthful courage, that a happy world of love quivers through me; I enjoy my existence only with you, only with you, only with you; I enjoy my existence only with you, only with you! Only with you does the breeze blow so soothingly for me, does the meadow seem so green to me, so gentle the blossoming of spring, so full of balm the evening, so cool the grove, only with you, so cool the grove, only with you, only with you! Only with you does pain lose its bitterness, does joy gain in pleasure! You make my heart secure in its ancestral inheritance; I feel that I belong to myself only with you, only with you, only with you! I feel that I belong to myself only with you, only with you, only with you!

Wiegenlied/Lullaby
(Seidl)

How the childlike heaven of the little eyes, laden with slumber, indolently closes! How the childlike heaven of the little eyes, laden with slumber, indolently closes! Close them that way on the day the earth calls you: inside is heaven, outside is pleasure! Inside is heaven, outside is pleasure! How your cheeks burn so red with sleep! Roses from Eden blew on them. How your cheeks burn so red with sleep! Roses from Eden blew on them: roses the cheeks, heaven the eyes, happy morning, heavenly day, happy morning, heavenly day! How the golden waves of your hair cool the glowing border of your temples! How the golden waves of your hair cool the glowing border of your temples! Beautiful is the hair of gold, more beautiful the wreath upon it: dream about laurel until it blooms for you; dream about laurel until it blooms for you. Lovely little mouth, angels hover around you; inside is innocence, inside is love. Lovely little mouth, angels hover around you; inside is innocence, inside is love. Guard them, my child, guard them faithfully: lips are roses, lips are flame, lips are roses, lips are flame. Just as an angel joins your hands together, join them that way on the day you go to rest! Just as an angel joins your hands together, join them that way on the day you go to rest! Beautiful are one's dreams when one has prayed: and your awakening repays you with the dream, and your awakening repays you with the dream.

Das Lied im Grünen/The Song in Nature's Greenness
(Reil)

Out into the greenness, out into the greenness; springtime, the lovely boy, beckons us there and leads us, leaning on a staff wound about with flowers, out where the larks and blackbirds are so lively, to the forests, to the fields, to hills, to the brook, into the greenness, into the greenness. In the greenness, in the greenness, life is blissful; we enjoy walking and even from afar we already turn our eyes in that direction; and as we walk in that way with a happy heart, childlike pleasure always surrounds us, in the greenness, in the greenness. In the greenness, in the greenness, we rest so well, we have such beautiful feelings and we think cozily about this and that, and we conjure away what, alas! depresses us, and we conjure everything that delights the heart toward us, everything toward us; and we conjure away what, alas! depresses us, and we conjure everything that delights the heart toward us, everything toward us, in the greenness, in the greenness. In the greenness, in the greenness, in the greenness, the stars become so clear—the stars that the sages of antiquity recommend to us as a guide to our existence. The little clouds sail by so gently for us, the little clouds sail by so gently for us, so gently for us, that our hearts grow happy and our mind grows clear, that our hearts grow happy and our mind grows clear, our mind grows clear, in the greenness, in the greenness. In the greenness, in the greenness, many a plan was borne aloft on wings, the future freed of a dismal prospect, your eyes grow strong, your gaze is refreshed, your wishes rock gently back and forth, in the greenness, in the greenness. In the greenness, in the greenness, in the morning, in the evening, in intimate silence, many a song and many an idyll germinate, and Hymen often crowns the poetical sport; for temptation comes easily, hearts are receptive in the greenness, in the greenness. Oh, even as a boy and youth I liked to be out in the greenness, and I learned, and wrote and read, in Horace and Plato, then Wieland and Kant, and with an ardent heart called myself blissful in the greenness, in the greenness. Into the greenness, into the greenness let us merrily follow the friendly boy! If one day life will no longer grow green for us, at any rate we wisely will not have missed the green time, and, when it mattered, we will at any rate have dreamed happily in the greenness, in the greenness. Let us merrily follow the friendly boy, let us merrily follow the friendly boy! If one day life will no longer grow green for us, at any rate we wisely will not have missed the green time, and, when it mattered, we will at any rate have dreamed happily, and, when it mattered, we will at any rate have dreamed happily in the greenness, in the greenness.

Der Kreuzzug / The Crusade
(Leitner)

A monk stands in his cell by the gray window lattice; many knights in bright armor ride through the field. They sing songs of a pious kind in beautiful, serious chorus; in their midst the banner of the Cross, of soft silk, the banner of the Cross, of soft silk, flies high. On the seashore they board the tall ship; it moves quickly away on its green path; soon it looks no bigger than a swan. The monk still stands at the window, gazes out after them: "I am still a pilgrim like you, even if I stay home. Life's journey through treacherous waves and hot desert sand is also a crusade to the Promised Land, to the Promised Land."

Der Winterabend / The Winter Evening
(Leitner)

It is so quiet, so cozy around me; the sun is down, the day has flown. How quickly the evening now becomes gray! I like it this way; at other times things are too loud for me. But now it is calm, no blacksmith is hammering, no plumber; the people have dispersed and are tired. And, so that the passing carts would not rattle, even the snow has spread blankets over the narrow streets, the snow has spread blankets over the narrow streets. How good this blessed peace is for me! I sit here in the dark, completely isolated, all by myself, all by myself. Only the moonlight comes softly, comes softly into my room. It knows me by now and permits me to remain silent; it merely takes up its handwork, the spindle, the gold, and quietly spins, weaves and smiles sweetly, and then hangs its glittering gauze all around on my furnishings and the walls. Its visit is truly a quiet and welcome one; it causes no commotion in my home. If the moonlight wants to stay, it has room; if it becomes dissatisfied, it goes away, it goes away. I then like to sit silently by the window, looking up at the clouds and stars. I think back, ah, far, really far, to a beautiful time that has disappeared. I think about her, about the happiness of love; I quietly sigh and meditate, and meditate, I quietly sigh and meditate. I think about her, about the

happiness of love; I quietly sigh and meditate, and meditate, I quietly sigh and meditate, and meditate and meditate.

Die Sterne / The Stars
(Leitner)

How brightly the stars flash through the night! I have often awakened from slumber because of them. I don't blame these bright figures for that; they perform many a salubrious duty in the silence, they perform many a salubrious duty in the silence. They drift high above in the form of angels, they light the pilgrim's way through heaths and forest. They hover round about as messengers of love, and often carry kisses far over the sea, and often carry kisses far over the sea. They look gently into the face of the sufferer, and put a border of silvery light on his tears. And, very consolingly and sweetly, they point the way for us with fingers of gold away from graves and out into the blue, out into the blue with fingers of gold. So bless you, then, you radiant troupe! And keep on shining for me, friendly and clear! And if I ever fall in love, be favorable to the union, be favorable to the union, and let your gleaming be our blessing, and let your gleaming be our blessing!

Auf dem Strom / On the River
(Rellstab)

Take the last farewell kisses and the wind-borne words that I still send to the riverbank before your feet turn away in parting! Already the boat is quickly drawn away by the waves of the river, but longing constantly draws back the tear-darkened gaze, it draws it, longing constantly draws it back! And so the billows bear me away with a speed I did not wish for. Ah, it has already disappeared, the meadow where I blissfully found her, ah, where I blissfully found her! Eternally gone, you days of rapture, eternally gone, you days of rapture! Emptied of hope it fades away, my lament for my beautiful native land, where I found her love, her love. See how the riverbanks speed by, and how I yearn to be upon them—how I am drawn by unnamable bonds—to land there by the cottage, to linger there in the arbor; but the river waves hasten further without rest or repose, hasten without rest or repose, they bear me on to the ocean, bear me on to the ocean. Ah, at the thought of that dark wilderness, far from any cheerful coast, where no island is to be seen, where no island is to be seen, oh, how I am seized by fearful trembling, oh, how I am seized by fearful trembling! No song can force its way from the shore to gently bring tears of melancholy; only the storm blows coldly past, only the storm blows coldly past, through the grayly mounting sea, through the grayly mounting sea! If my yearningly roaming eyes can no longer light upon a shore, well, then, now I look up to the stars in those hallowed distant spaces! Ah, by their gentle light I first called her mine; there, perhaps, o happy consolation! there I will meet her gaze, there, there I will meet her gaze. By the stars' gentle light I first called her mine; there, perhaps, o happy consolation! there I will meet her gaze; there, perhaps, o happy consolation! there I will meet her gaze, there I will meet her gaze, there I will meet her gaze.

Der Hirt auf dem Felsen.
Nach Wilh. Müller's Gedicht "Der Berghirt"
The Shepherd on the Rock.
Adapted from *Wilhelm Müller's* poem
"The Mountain Shepherd"

When I stand on the highest crag and look down into the deep valley, and sing, and sing: distantly from the deep, dark valley the echo flies up, the echo of the ravines. The further my voice travels, the more brightly it echoes back to me from below, from below. My sweetheart lives so far from me; that's why I long so ardently to join her there, to join her there. The further my voice travels, the more brightly it echoes back to me from below, from below. When I stand on the highest crag and look down into the deep valley, and sing, and sing: distantly from the deep, dark valley the echo flies up, the echo of the ravines. I am consumed by deep sorrow; my joy has departed; all my hopes on earth are gone; I am so lonely here, I am so lonely here. Thus longingly resounded the song in the forest, thus longingly it resounded through the night; it draws all hearts heavenward with magical power, it draws all hearts heavenward with magical power. Spring is about to come, spring, my joy; now I shall prepare for a long walking journey, now I shall prepare for a long walking journey. Spring is about to come, o spring, my joy; spring is about to come, spring, my joy; now I shall prepare for a long walking journey. The further my voice travels, the more brightly it echoes back to me; the further my voice travels, the more brightly it echoes back to me. The further my voice travels, the further my voice travels, the more brightly, the more brightly it echoes back to me. Spring is about to come, spring is about to come, spring, my joy; now I shall prepare for a long walking journey. Spring is about to come, spring, my joy; spring is about to come, spring, my joy; now I shall prepare for a long walking journey. The further my voice travels, the more brightly it echoes back to me; the further my voice travels, the more brightly it echoes back to me; the further my voice travels, the more brightly it echoes back to me, the more brightly it echoes back to me.

Des Mädchens Klage.

Gedicht von Fr. v. Schiller.

Für eine Singstimme mit Begleitung des Pianoforte

componirt von

FRANZ SCHUBERT.

Zweite Fassung.

Op. 58. № 3.

1

bricht sich die Wel - le mit Macht, mit Macht, und sie seufzt hin -
Hei - li - ge, ru - fe dein Kind zu - rück, ich ha - be ge -
sü - sse - ste Glück für die trau - ern - de Brust nach der schö - nen

aus ____ in die fin - st're Nacht, das Au - ge vom Wei - nen ge -
nos - sen das ir - dische Glück, ich ha - be ge - lebt ____ und ge -
Lie - be ver - schwund - ner ____ Lust, ich, die Himm - li - sche, will's ____ nicht ver -
Lie - be ver - schwund - ner ____ Lust sind der Lie - be Schmer - zen und

trü - - bet.
lie - - bet!"
sa - - gen.
Kla - - gen.

Hoffnung.

Gedicht von Fr. v. Schiller.

Für eine Singstimme mit Begleitung des Pianoforte
componirt von

FRANZ SCHUBERT.

7. August 1815.

Es re_den und träu_men die Men_schen viel von bes_sern künf_ti_gen Ta___gen; nach ei_nem_ glück_li_chen, gol_de_nen Ziel sieht man sie ren_nen und ja___gen. Die

3

Welt wird alt und wird wie - der_ jung, doch der Mensch hofft

im - mer Ver-bes - se - rung, doch der Mensch hofft

im - mer Ver-bes - se - rung.

Die Hoffnung führt ihn ins Leben ein,
    Sie umflattert den fröhlichen Knaben,
Den Jüngling lockt ihr Zauberschein,
    Sie wird mit dem Greis nicht begraben;
Denn beschliesst er im Grabe den müden Lauf,
Noch am Grabe pflanzt er die Hoffnung auf.

Es ist kein leerer, schmeichelnder Wahn,
    Erzeugt im Gehirne des Thoren.
Im Herzen kündet es laut sich an:
    Zu was Besserem sind wir geboren;
Und was die innere Stimme spricht,
Das täuscht die hoffende Seele nicht.

4

An den Frühling.

Gedicht von Fr. v. Schiller.

Für eine Singstimme mit Begleitung des Pianoforte
componirt von

FRANZ SCHUBERT.

Zweite Fassung.

October 1817.

auf _____ der Flur! Ei! ei! Da bist_ ja wie _ der! Und
liebt _____ mich noch! Für's Mäd _ chen man _ ches Blüm _ chen er _

bist so_ lieb und schön! Und freun wir uns_ so herz _ lich, ent _
bat ich mir von dir_ ich_ komm' und bit _ te wie _ der, und_

cresc.   *p*

ge _ gen dir_ zu gehn, ent _ ge _ gen dir_ zu gehn.
du? Du giebst es mir, und_ du?_ Du giebst es_ mir.

p

Dem Unendlichen.

Gedicht von Fr. G. Klopstock.

Für eine Singstimme mit Begleitung des Pianoforte
componirt von

FRANZ SCHUBERT.

Zweite Fassung.

Al_lein du rufst mich aus meiner Nacht, der im E _ lend, der im To _ de hilft!

Dann denk' ich es ganz, dass du e _ wig mich schufst, Herr _ licher, den kein Preis, unten am

Grab, o _ ben am Thron, Herr _ Gott, den, dankend entflammt, kein Ju _ bel ge _ nug be _

Langsam, mit aller Kraft.

singt! Weht, Bäu _ _ _ me des Le _ bens, in's

Har _ _ _ fen ge _ tön'! Rau _ sche mit ih _ nen in's Har _ fenge _ tön', kry _ stall' _ _ ner_ Strom! Ihr lis _ _ pelt und rauscht, und, Har _ _ fen, ihr tönt nie es ganz: Gott_ ist es, Gott_ ist es, den ihr preist. Wel _ _ ten, don _ nert in

hal - - lest nie _____ es ganz: Gott, nie_

_ es ganz: Gott, Gott, _____ Gott _____

_ ist es, den ihr

preist!

An den Mond.

Gedicht von L.H.Chr.Hölty.

Für eine Singstimme mit Begleitung des Pianoforte
componirt von

FRANZ SCHUBERT.

7. August 1816.

Was schau_est du so hell und klar durch die_se Ap_fel_bäu_me, wo
Du blickst umsonst so hell und klar in die_se Lau_be nie_der; nie
O wan_delt sie hin_fort ein_mal an mei_ner Ru_he_stel_le, dann

einst dein Freund so se_lig_war und träum_te süs_se Träu_me? Ver_
fin_dest du das fro_he_Paar in ih_rem Schat_ten wie_der! Ein
ma_che flugs mit trü_bem Strahl des Gra_bes Blu_men hel_le! Sie

hül_le dei_nen Sil_berglanz, und schimm_re, wie du schim_merst, wenn du den frü_hen
schwar_zes feind_li_ches Geschick ent_riss mir mei_ne Schö_ne! Kein Seuf_zer zau_bert
set_ze wei_nend sich aufs Grab, wo Ro_sen nie_der_han_gen, und pflü_cke sich ein

To_dtenkranz der jun_gen Braut be_flim_merst!
sie zu_rück, und kei_ne_Sehnsuchts_thrä_ne!
Blüm_chen ab, und drück' es_ an die Wan_gen.

cresc.

12

Der Wanderer.

Gedicht von Schmidt von Lübeck.

Für eine Singstimme mit Begleitung des Pianoforte

componirt von

FRANZ SCHUBERT.

Op. 4. Nº 1.

Dem Patriarchen Joh. Ladisl. Pyrker v. Felsö-Eör gewidmet.

fragt der Seuf _ zer wo? im _ mer wo? Die Son _ ne dünkt mich hier so __ kalt, die

Blü _ the welk, das Le _ ben alt, und was sie re _ den lee _ rer Schall, ich bin ein Fremdling

Etwas geschwinder.

ü _ berall. Wo bist du, wo bist du, mein ge _ lieb _ tes Land? ge_

sucht, __ ge _ ahnt, __ und nie __ ge_

Geschwind.

kannt. Das Land, das Land so hoffnungsgrün, so hoffnungsgrün, das Land, wo mei _ ne

Ro_senblühn, wo mei_ne Freunde wan_delndgehn, wo mei_ne To_dten auf_er_stehn, das

cresc. *f*

Wie anfangs, sehr langsam.

Land,dasmei_ne Spra_chespricht, o Land, _ wo bistdu?

fp *fp* *pp* *dim.*

Ich wan_dle _ still, bin we_nig froh, und im_mer

fragt der Seuf_zer wo? im_mer wo? Im Gei_sterhauch tönt's

ppp

mir zu_rück: Dort wo du nichtbist, dort ist das Glück.

fp

Lied eines Schiffers an die Dioskuren.

Von Joh. Mayrhofer.

Für eine Singstimme mit Begleitung des Pianoforte

componirt von

FRANZ SCHUBERT.

Op. 65. № 1.

1816.

fühlt sich doch in eu_ren Strah_len dop_pelt mu_thig und ge_seg_

net. Die_ses Ru_der, das ich schwin_ge, Mee_res_

flu_then zu zer_thei_len, hän_ge ich, so ich ge_

bor_gen, auf an eu_res Tem_pels Säu_len, Di_os_ku_ren, Zwil_lings_

ster_ne!

Wiegenlied

von M. Claudius.(?)

Für eine Singstimme mit Begleitung des Pianoforte

componirt von

FRANZ SCHUBERT.

Op. 98. Nº 2.

November 1816.

Abendlied

von M. Claudius.

Für eine Singstimme mit Begleitung des Pianoforte

componirt von

FRANZ SCHUBERT.

November 1816.

stei _ _ get der wei _ sse Ne _ bel wun _ der _ bar.
Jam _ _ mer ver schla _ fen und _ ver _ ges _ sen sollt.

Seht ihr den Mond dort stehen?
Er ist nur halb zu sehen,
   Und ist doch rund und schön!
So sind wohl manche Sachen,
Die wir getrost belachen,
   Weil unsre Augen sie nicht sehn.

Wir stolze Menschenkinder
Sind eitel arme Sünder,
   Und wissen gar nicht viel.
Wir spinnen Luftgespinnste,
Und suchen viele Künste
   Und kommen weiter von dem Ziel.

Gott, lass dein Heil uns schauen,
Auf nichts Vergänglichs trauen,
   Nicht Eitelkeit uns freun!
Lass uns einfältig werden,
Und vor dir hier auf Erden
   Wie Kinder fromm und fröhlich sein.

Der Tod und das Mädchen.

Gedicht von M. Claudius.

Für eine Singstimme mit Begleitung des Pianoforte

componirt von

FRANZ SCHUBERT.

Op. 7. № 3.

Dem Grafen Ludw. Széchényi von Sarvári-Felsö-Vidék gewidmet.

Februar 1817.

Vor_ü_ber, ach vor_über, geh' wil_der Kno_chenmann! Ich bin noch jung, geh' Lie_ber, und rühre mich nicht an, und rühre mich nicht an. Gieb deine Hand, du schön und zart Ge_bild, bin Freund, und kom_me nicht zu_ stra_fen. Sei gutes Muths! ich bin nicht wild, sollst sanft in meinen Armen schla_fen.

An die Musik.

Gedicht von Fr. v. Schober.

Für eine Singstimme mit Begleitung des Pianoforte

componirt von

FRANZ SCHUBERT.

Zweite Fassung.

Op. 88. No 4.

Die Forelle.

Gedicht von Chr. Fr. D. Schubart.

Für eine Singstimme mit Begleitung des Pianoforte

componirt von

FRANZ SCHUBERT.

Vierte Fassung.

Op. 32.

In ei_nem Bächlein hel _ _ le da schoss in fro_her Eil' die
Fi_scher mit der Ru _ _ the wohl an dem U_fer stand, und

lau _ ni_sche Fo_rel _ _ le vor_ü_ber_ wie ein Pfeil. Ich
sah's mit kal_tem Blu _ te, wie sich das_ Fischlein wand. So

stand an dem Ge_sta _ _ de und sah in sü_sser Ruh' des
lang dem Was_ser Hel _ _ le, so dacht' ich, nicht ge_bricht, so

mun_tern Fischleins Ba _ _ de im kla _ ren Bächlein zu, des
fängt er die Fo_rel _ _ le mit sei_ner An_gel nicht, so

mun - tern Fischleins Ba _ _ de im kla _ ren Bächlein zu.
fängt er die Fo - rel _ _ le mit sei _ ner An - gel nicht.

Ein

Doch end - lich ward dem Die _ _ be die Zeit zu

lang, er macht das Bäch - lein tü - ckisch trü _ _ be, und

eh' _____ ich es ge_dacht, so zuck_te sei _ ne Ru_the, das

Fisch _ lein, das Fisch_lein zap _ pelt d'ran, und ich mit re_gem

Blu _ _ te sah die Be_trog'ne an, und ich_ mit re _ gem

Blu _ _ te sah die Be_trog'ne an.

25

Gruppe aus dem Tartarus.

Gedicht von Fr. v. Schiller.

Für eine Singstimme mit Begleitung des Pianoforte

componirt von

FRANZ SCHUBERT.

Op. 24. № 1.

September 1817.

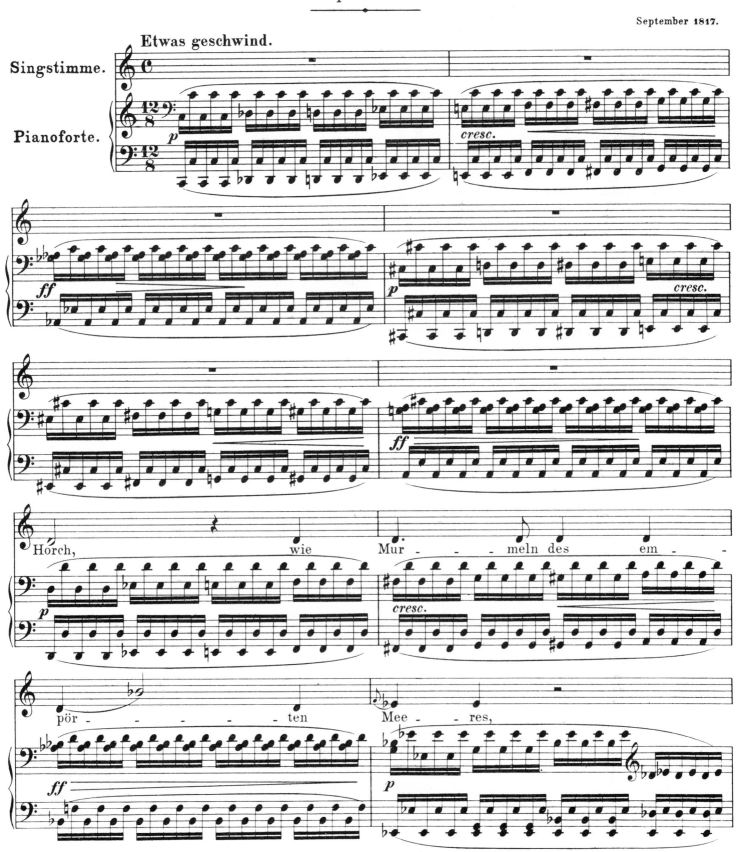

wie durch hoh - - ler Fel - - sen Be - - cken

weint _____ ein Bach,

stöhnt dort dum - - pfig - tief ein

schwe - - res, lee - - res,

qual - - - - er - press - - - - - tes

Allegro.

Ach! Schmerz ver _ zer _ ret ihr __ Ge _ sicht; Ver _ zweif _ lung

sper _ ret ihren Ra _ chen flu _ chend auf. Hohl sind ih _ re

Au _ gen, ih _ re Bli _ cke spä _ hen bang nach des Co _ cy _ tus Brü _ cke, fol _ gen

thrä _ nend sei _ nem Trau _ er _ lauf, sei _ nem Trau _ er _ lauf.

Fragen sich einander ängstlich lei _ se, ob noch

Sen - se des Sa - turns ent - zwei. E - - wig-

keit schwingt ü - ber ih - - - nen Krei - se, bricht die

Sen - se des Sa - turns ent - zwei, bricht die

Sen - se des Sa - turns ent - zwei.

Der Alpenjäger.

Gedicht von Fr. v. Schiller.

Für eine Singstimme mit Begleitung des Pianoforte

componirt von

FRANZ SCHUBERT.

Op. 37. № 2.

L. F. Schnorr von Karolsfeld gewidmet.

October 1817.

Willst du_ nicht das Lämm_lein hü_ten? Lämm_lein ist_ so fromm und_ sanft,
Willst du_ nicht die Heer_de lo_cken mit_ des Hor_nes mun_term Klang?
Willst du_ nicht der Blüm_lein war_ten, die_ im Bee_te freund_lich_ stehn?

nährt sich_ von des Gra_ses Blü_then, spie_lend an_ des Ba_ches Ranft.
Lieb_lich_ tönt der Schall_ der Glo_cken in_ des Wal_des Lust_ge_sang.
Drau_ssen_ la_det dich_ kein Gar_ten, wild_ ist's auf_ den wil_den Höhn!

Geschwind.

Mut_ter, Mut_ter lass mich ge_hen, ja_gen nach des Ber_ges
Mut_ter, Mut_ter lass mich ge_hen, schweifen auf den wil_den
Lass die Blümlein, lass sie blü_hen, Mut_ter, Mut_ter, lass mich

Höhen, ja - gen nach des Ber - ges Höh'n!
Höhen, schweifen auf den wil - den Höh'n!
zie - hen, Mut - ter, Mut - ter lass mich ziehn!

ritard.

Geschwind.

Und der Kna - be ging zu ja - gen, und es treibt und reisst ihn fort, rast - los fort mit blin - dem
Auf der Fel - sen nack - te Rippen klet - tert sie mit leich - tem Schwung, durch den Riss gespalt'ner
Je - tzo auf den schroffen Zinken hängt sie, auf dem höchsten Grat, wo die Fel - sen jäh ver -

Wa - gen an des Ber - ges finstern Ort; vor ihm her mit Win - des - schnel - le flieht die
Klippen trägt sie der ge - wag - te Sprung; a - ber hin - ter ihr ver - wo - gen folgt er
sinken, und ver - schwunden ist der Pfad; un - ter sich die stei - le Hö - he, hin - ter

zit - tern - de Ga - zel - le.
mit dem To - des - bo - gen.
sich des Fein - des Nä - he.

Mit des Jammers stummen Blicken fleht sie zu dem har-ten Mann, fleht um-sonst, denn los-zu-

drücken legt er schon den Bogen an. **Langsam.** Plötzlich aus der Felsen-spal-te tritt der

Geist, der Berges-al-te. Und mit sei-nen Göt-ter-händen schützt er das gequäl-te

Thier. „Musst du Tod und Jammer senden," ruft er, „bis herauf zu mir? Raum für Al-le hat die

Er-de; was verfolgst du meine Heer-de, was verfolgst du meine Heer-de?"

Litaney
auf das Fest Aller Seelen.
Von J. G. Jacobi.
Für eine Singstimme mit Begleitung des Pianoforte
componirt von
FRANZ SCHUBERT.

August 1818

nie _ en, denn in je _ nen Tö _ nen lebt es.

Nur die Nach _ ti _ gall kann __ sa _ gen, wie er in _ nig sich mir giebt, um zu

lin _ dern mei _ ne Kla _ gen, dass er nicht so in _ nig liebt, dass er

nicht so in _ nig liebt.

Sehnsucht.

Gedicht von Fr. v. Schiller.

Für eine Singstimme mit Begleitung des Pianoforte
componirt von

FRANZ SCHUBERT.

Zweite Fassung.

Op. 39.

Ziemlich geschwind.

Singstimme.

Pianoforte.

Ach, aus die _ ses Tha _ les Gründen, die der
kal _ te Ne _ bel drückt, könnt' ich doch den Aus _ gang fin _ den,
ach, wie fühlt' ich mich be _ glückt, ach, wie fühlt' ich mich be _ glückt!

Dort er-blick'ich schö-ne Hü-gel, e-wig jung und e-wig grün! Hätt' ich Schwingen, hätt' ich Flü-gel, nach den Hü-geln zög' ich hin, nach den Hü-geln zög' ich hin.

Harmo-nie-en hör' ich klingen, Tö-ne süsser

Himmelsruh, _____ und die leich _ ten Win _ de bringen mir der Düf _ te Bal _ sam

zu. Gold' _ ne Früchte seh' ich glühen, win _ kend zwischen dun _ kelm Laub,

winkend zwischen dun _ kelm Laub, und die Blu _ _ men, die dort blü _ hen,

wer _ den kei _ nes Win _ ters Raub, wer _ den kei _ nes Win _ ters Raub.

Ach, wie schön muss sich's er ge hen

dort im ew' gen Son nen schein! Und die Luft auf je nen

Hö hen, o wie la bend muss sie sein!

Doch mir wehrt des Stro mes

To _ ben, der er _ grimmt da _ zwi _ _ schen braust; sei _ ne

Wel _ _ len sind ge _ ho _ ben, dass die See _ _ le mir er _

graust. Ei _ nen

Na _ _ chen seh' ich schwan _ ken, a _ ber ach! der _____

Fähr _ _ _ mann fehlt!

Schnell.

Frisch hin ein, und oh ne Wanken! Seine Se gel sind beseelt, seine Se gel sind beseelt,

frisch hin ein, und oh ne Wanken! Du musst glau ben,

du musst wa gen, denn die Göt ter leih'n kein Pfand;

nur ein Wun der kann dich tra gen in das schö ne Wun derland.

45

Du musst glau _ ben, du _ musst wa _ gen, denn die Göt _ _ ter

leih'n _ kein Pfand; nur ein Wun _ der kann dich tra _ gen

in das schö_ne Wun_derland, in das schö _ ne_

Wun _ _ _ der _ land.

Der Jüngling am Bache.

Gedicht von Fr. v. Schiller.

Für eine Singstimme mit Begleitung des Pianoforte

componirt von

FRANZ SCHUBERT.

Ursprüngliche Fassung.

April 1819.

Singstimme.

Pianoforte.

An der Quel_le sass der Kna_be, Blu_ men wand er sich zum

Fra_ get nicht, wa_ rum ich trau_re in des Le _ bens Blüthen_

Kranz, Blu_ men wand er_ sich zum Kranz, und er sah sie, fort ge_

zeit, in des Le_ bens Blü_ then_ zeit! Al_les freu _ et sich und

ris_ sen, trei_ben in der Wel_ len Tanz, trei_ben in_ der Wel_ len

hof_ fet, wenn der Früh_ ling sich er _ neut, wenn der Früh_ ling sich er_

Tanz. Und so flie_hen mei_ne Ta_ge, wie die Quel_le,rast_los
neut. A_ber die_se tau_send Stim_men der er_wa_chenden Na_

hin! Und so blei_chet mei_ne Ju_gend, wie die
tur we_cken in dem tie_fen Bu_sen mir den

Krän_ze schnell ver_blühn, wie die Krän_ze_ schnell ver_blühn!
schwe_ren Kum_mer nur, mir den schwe_ren Kum_mer nur.

Was soll mir dir Freude frommen,
　Die der schöne Lenz mir beut?
Eine nur ist's, die ich suche,
　Sie ist nah und ewig weit.
Sehnend breit' ich meine Arme
　Nach dem theuren Schattenbild,
Ach, ich kann es nicht erreichen,
　Und das Herz bleibt ungestillt.

Komm herab, du schöne Holde,
　Und verlass dein stolzes Schloss!
Blumen, die der Lenz geboren,
　Streu' ich dir in deinen Schooss.
Horch, der Hain erschallt von Liedern,
　Und die Quelle rieselt klar!
Raum ist in der kleinsten Hütte
　Für ein glücklich liebend Paar.

Nachtstück.

Gedicht von Joh. Mayrhofer.

Für eine Singstimme mit Begleitung des Pianoforte

componirt von

FRANZ SCHUBERT.

In C moll Op. 36. № 2.

Frau Katharina von Lacsny gewidmet,

October 1819.

Wenn über Berge sich der Ne_bel brei_tet, und Lu_na mit Ge_wölken kämpft; so nimmt der Al_te sei_ne Har_fe, und schrei_tet und singt wald_ein_wärts und ge_dämpft: „Du heil'_ _ _ge

mer.   Du heil' _ _ ge Nacht!   Bald

ist's   voll _ bracht. Bald schlaf' ich ihn, den

lan _ _ _ _ _ gen Schlum _ _ mer,   der

mich er _ löst _ von al _ _ lem Kum _ mer, der

mich er _ löst _ von al _ _ lem Kum _ _ _

mer. Die

grü _ _ nen Bäu _ me rau _ _ schen dann: Schlaf'

süss, du gu _ ter _ al _ _ ter Mann; die

Grä _ _ _ ser lis _ peln wan _ _ kend fort:_____ Wir

de _ _ _ cken sei _ _ nen Ru _ _ he _ ort; die

52

grü — — nen Bäu — me ____ rau — schen dann: Schlaf

süss, du gu — ter ____ al — — ter Mann; und

man — — cher lie — — be Vo — — gel ruft: ____ O

lass ihn ruhn ____ in ____ Ra — — sengruft, o

lass ihn ruhn ____ in ____ Ra — — sengruft!"

Der Al - te horcht,

der Al - te schweigt

Der Tod hat sich zu

ihm ge-neigt, der Tod hat sich zu

ihm ge-neigt.

Die Vögel.

Gedicht von Fr. Schlegel.

Für eine Singstimme mit Begleitung des Pianoforte

componirt von

FRANZ SCHUBERT.

Erschienen als Op. 172. № 6.

Sie jammern in Nö_then, wir flat_tern gen Him_mel, wir flat _ tern gen Him_mel.

Der Jä_ger will tö_dten, dem Früch _ te wir pick_ten;____

wir müs_sen ihn höh_nen, und Beu _ te ge _ win _ nen.____

Frühlingsglaube.

Gedicht von L. Uhland.

Für eine Singstimme mit Begleitung des Pianoforte

componirt von

FRANZ SCHUBERT.

Zweite Fassung.

Op. 20. № 2.

Frau Justina von Bruchmann gewidmet.

November 1822.

neu _ er Klang! Nun, ar_mes Her_ze, sei nicht bang, nun muss sich al _ les,

al _ _ les wen _ den, nun muss sich al _ les, al _ les wen _ den.

Die

Welt wird schö_ner mit je _ dem Tag, man weiss nicht, was_ noch wer_den mag, das

Blü _ hen will nicht en _ _ den, es_ will nicht en _ _ den. Es

blüht das_ fern_ste, tief_ste Thal, es blüht das

tief_ste Thal, nun, ar_mes Herz ver_giss der Qual,

nun muss sich al_les, al_les wen_den, nun muss sich al_les,

al_les wen_den.

Der Jüngling an der Quelle.

Gedicht von J. G. v. Salis.

Für eine Singstimme mit Begleitung des Pianoforte

componirt von

FRANZ SCHUBERT.

1821.

Lei _ se, rie _ selnder Quell, ihr wal _ lenden, flis _ pernden Pap _ peln, eu _ er Schlum _ mer _ ge _ räusch we _ cket die Lie _ be nur auf.

Lin _ derung sucht' ich bei euch, und sie zu ver _ ges _ sen, die

Sprö _ de; ach, und Blät _ ter und Bach seuf _ zen: Lu _ i _ se! mir

zu, ach,___ und Blät _ ter und Bach seuf _ zen: Lu _

i _ _ _ se! mir zu. Lu _ i _ _ _ _

se! Lu _ i _ _ se!

Sei mir gegrüsst!

Gedicht von Fr. Rückert.

Für eine Singstimme mit Begleitung des Pianoforte

componirt von

FRANZ SCHUBERT.

Op. 20. Nº 1.

Frau Justina von Bruchmann gewidmet.

sei mir ge_grüsst, sei mir ge_küsst, sei mir ge_küsst!

Du von der Hand der Lie _ be die_sem Her _ zen Ge_geb' _ ne!

du, von dieser Brust _____ Ge _ nomm' _ ne mir! mit die _ sem Thränen _ gus _ se

sei mir ge_grüsst, sei mir ge_küsst, sei mir ge_

küsst! Zum Trotz der Fer _ ne, die sich, feind_lich tren _ nend,

hat zwischen mich und dich gestellt; dem Neid der Schicksals-mäch - te zum Ver - drus - se

sei mir ge - grüsst, sei mir ge - küsst, sei mir ge -

küsst! Wie du mir je___ im schön - sten Lenz der

Lie - be mit Gruss und Kuss___ ent - ge - gen kamst, mit mei - ner

See___ le glü - hendstem Er - gus - se sei mir ge - grüsst,

sei mir ge_küsst, sei mir ge_küsst! Ein Hauch der

Lie _ _ be til _ get Räum' und Zei _ ten, ich bin bei dir,

du bist bei mir,_____ ich hal _ te dich in dieses Arms_____ Um_

schlus _ _ se, sei mir ge_grüsst, sei mir ge_

küsst, sei mir ge _ küsst!_____

Selige Welt.

Gedicht von Joh. Senn.

Für eine Bassstimme mit Begleitung des Pianoforte

componirt von

FRANZ SCHUBERT.

Op. 23. No 2.

Ei_ne se _ li_ge In_sel sucht der Wahn,   ei_ne

se _ li_ge In_sel sucht der Wahn,   doch ei _ ne ist es nicht,   doch ei _ ne ist es

nicht.   Du lan _ de _ gläu_big ü _ ber_all an,

ü_ber_all an,   wo sich Was_ser an Er_de bricht.

Schwanengesang.

Gedicht von Joh. Senn.

Für eine Singstimme mit Begleitung des Pianoforte

componirt von

FRANZ SCHUBERT.

Op. 23. № 3.

Wie klag' ich's aus das Ster_be_ge_fühl, das auf_lö_send durch die Glie_der rinnt, wie sing' ich's aus das Wer_de_gefühl,

das er _ lö _ send dich, o Geist, an _ weht. Er

klagt', er sang ver _ nich _ tungs _ bang, ver _ klä _ rungs _ froh,

bis das_ Le _ ben_ floh.

Das_____ be _ deu _ tet des Schwa _ nen Ge _ sang.

An die Leyer.

Gedicht (nach Anakreon) von Fr. Bruchmann.

Für eine Singstimme mit Begleitung des Pianoforte

componirt von

FRANZ SCHUBERT.

Op. 56. N? 2.

Seinem Freunde Carl Pinterics gewidmet.

Tempo I.

Langsamer.

Doch auch die Sai_ten tö_nen nur Lie_be im Er_

klin_gen, doch auch die Sai_ten tö_nen nur Lie_be im Er_

klin_____gen. So lebt denn

wohl, He_ro_____en, denn mei_ne Sai_ten

tö_nen, statt Hel_densang zu dro_hen, nur Lie_be im Er_

klin - - - gen. So lebt denn wohl, He -

ro - - - en, denn mei - ne Sai - ten

tö - nen, statt Hel - den-sang zu dro - hen, nur

Lie - be im Er - klin - - - gen.

Der Zwerg.

Gedicht von Matth. v. Collin.

Für eine Singstimme mit Begleitung des Pianoforte

componirt von

FRANZ SCHUBERT.

Op. 22. № 1.

Dem Dichter gewidmet.

Schiff auf glat _ ten Mee _ res _ wo _ gen, wo _ rauf die Kö _ nigin mit

ih _ rem Zwer _ ge.

Sie schaut em _

por zum hoch _ ge _ wölb _ ten _ Bo _ gen, hin _

auf zur lichtdurchwirkten blau _ en Fer _ ne, die mit der Milch des Himmels blass durch _ zo _

gen. Nie, nie habt ihr mir ge_lo_gen noch, ihr

Ster_ne, so ruft sie aus, bald werd' ich nun ent_schwin_den, ihr sagt es mir, doch

sterb'_____ ich wahrlich ger_ne. Da tritt der Zwerg zur

Kö_nigin, mag bin_den um ihren Hals die Schnur von rother Sei_de, und weint, und

weint, als wollt' er schnell vor Gram er_blin_den, vor Gram erblin_den. Er spricht: Du

selbst bist Schuld an diesem Lei _ de, weil um den König du mich hast ver _ las _ sen, jetzt weckt dein

Ster _ ben einzig mir noch Freu _ de, ein _ zig mir noch Freu _ de. Zwar werd'ich e _ wiglich mich

sel _ ber has _ _ sen, der dir mit die _ ser Hand den

Tod ge _ ge _ _ ben, doch musst zum frü _ hen Grab du

nun er blas _ _ sen.

Sie legt die Hand auf's Herz voll jun __ __ gem Le __ __ ben, und aus dem Aug' die schwe_ren Thränen rin _ nen, das sie zum Him_mel betend will er_he _ ben. Mögst du nicht Schmerz durch mei _ nen Tod ge _ win _ _ nen! sie sagt's, da küsst der

Zwerg die blei _ chen Wan_gen, d'rauf al _ so_bald_____ ver_ge _ hen ihr die Sin _ nen.

Der Zwerg schaut an die Frau, vom Tod be _ fan _ gen, er senkt sie tief in's Meer mit eig'nen Han _ den. Ihm brennt nach ihr das Herz so voll Ver_lan _ gen, ihm brennt nach ihr das Herz so

voll Ver lan _ _ gen, so voll Ver _ _

lan _ _ _ gen.

An kei _ _ ner Kü _ ste wird

er je mehr lan _ _

_ _ _ den.

Wehmuth.

Gedicht von Matth. v. Collin.

Für eine Singstimme mit Begleitung des Pianoforte

componirt von

FRANZ SCHUBERT.

Op. 22. № 2.

Dem Dichter gewidmet.

Auf dem Wasser zu singen.

Lied von Fr. L. Grafen zu Stolberg.

Für eine Singstimme mit Begleitung des Pianoforte

componirt von

FRANZ SCHUBERT.

Op. 72.

1823.

Mässig geschwind.

Singstimme.

Pianoforte.

Mit _ ten im Schim _ mer der spie _ geln _ den Wel _ len glei _ tet, wie Schwä _ ne, der
Ü _ ber den Wip _ feln des west _ li _ chen Hai _ nes win _ ket uns freundlich der
Ach, es ent _ schwin _ det mit thau _ i _ gem Flü _ gel mir auf den wie _ gen _ den

wan _ ken _ de Kahn; ach, auf der Freu _ de sanft _ schimmernden Wel _ len glei _ tet die See _ le da _
röth _ li _ che Schein; un _ ter den Zwei _ gen des öst _ li _ chen Hai _ nes säu _ selt der Cal _ mus im
Wel _ len die Zeit; morgen entschwin _ de mit schimmerndem Flü _ gel wie _ der wie ge _ stern und

hin wie der Kahn; ach, auf der Freu_de sanft=schimmernden Wel_len glei_tet die See_le da_
röth_li_chen Schein; un_ter den Zwei_gen des öst_li_chen Hai_nes säu_selt der Cal_mus im
heu_te die Zeit; mor_gen entschwin_de mit schimmerndem Flü_gel wie_der wie ge_stern und

hin wie der Kahn; denn von dem Him_mel her_ab auf die Wel_len
röth_li_chen Schein; Freu_de des Him_mels und Ru_he des Hai_nes
heu_te die Zeit, bis ich auf hö_he_rem strah_len_den Flü_gel

tan_zet das A_bendroth rund um den Kahn, tan_ _ _ _ _ _ _zet das
ath_met die Seel' im er_rö_thenden Schein, ath_ _ _ _ _ _ _met die
sel_ber entschwinde der wech_selnden Zeit, sel_ _ _ _ _ _ _ber ent_

A_bendroth rund um den Kahn.
Seel' im er_rö_thenden Schein.
schwinde der wechselnden Zeit.

Der Pilgrim.

Gedicht von Fr. v. Schiller.

Für eine Singstimme mit Begleitung des Pianoforte
componirt von

FRANZ SCHUBERT.

In D dur: Op. 37. № 1.

L. F. Schnorr von Karolsfeld gewidmet.

Mai **1823**.

Noch in mei_nes Le_bens Lenze war ich, und ich wan_dert' aus, und der Jugend fro_he Tänze liess ich in des Vaters Haus.

All mein Erb_theil, meine Habe warf ich fröhlich glau_bend hin, und am leichten

Pil_ger_sta_be zog ich fort mit Kindersinn.

Denn mich trieb ein

mäch_tig Hof_fen und ein dunk_les Glau_bens_wort, wand_le, rief's, der Weg ist of_fen,

immer nach dem Aufgang fort.

Bis zu ei_ner goldnen Pforten

du gelangst, da gehst du_ein, denn das Ir_di_sche wird dorten himmlisch, un_ver_gänglich sein.

A_bend ward's und wurde Morgen, nimmer, nim_mer stand ich still,

a ─ ber immer blieb's verbor ─ gen, was ich su ─ che, was ich will. Ber ─ ge la ─ gen mir im We ─ ge,

Strö ─ me hemmten mei ─ nen Fuss, ü ─ ber Schlünde baut' ich Ste ─ ge, Brü ─ cken durch den

wil ─ den Fluss. Und zu ei ─ nes Stroms Ge ─ sta ─ den kam ich, der nach

Mor ─ gen floss; froh ver ─ trau ─ end sei ─ nem Fa ─ den, warf ich mich in ─ sei ─ nen Schooss.

Hin zu ei ─ nem grossen Mee ─ re trieb mich sei ─ ner

Wel_len Spiel; vor mir liegt's in wei_ter Lee_re, vor mir liegt's in wei_ter Lee_re,

nä_her bin ich nicht dem ___ Ziel, nä_her bin ich nicht dem

Sehr langsam.

Ziel. _____ Ach, kein Weg will da_hin füh_ren, ach, der

Him_mel ü_ber mir_ will die Er_de nie be_rüh_ren, und das Dort ist niemals

hier, ist niemals hier, und das Dort ist niemals hier, ist niemals hier!

Dass sie hier gewesen.

Gedicht von Friedr. Rückert.

Für eine Singstimme mit Begleitung des Pianoforte

componirt von

FRANZ SCHUBERT.

Op. 59. № 2.

Singstimme.

Pianoforte.

Sehr langsam.

Dass der Ostwind Düf_te hau _ chet in die Lüf _ te,

dadurch thut er _ kund,_____ dass du hier ge _ we _ sen, dass du hier ge _ we _ sen.

Dass hier Thränen rin_nen, da _ durch wirst du in _ nen,

wär's dir sonst nicht kund,_____ dass ich hier ge _ we _ sen, dass ich hier ge_

Du bist die Ruh.

Gedicht von Fr. Rückert.

Für eine Singstimme mit Begleitung des Pianoforte

componirt von

FRANZ SCHUBERT.

Op. 59. № 3.

1823.

mein Aug' und— Herz.——

Kehr' ein bei mir, und schlie_sse du still hin _ ter

dir die Pfor _ ten zu. Treib' an _ dern Schmerz— aus die_ser—

Brust! Voll sei dies Herz— von dei_ner— Lust,— von dei_ner—

Lust.——

Dies Au - gen - zelt, von dei - nem Glanz al - lein er -

hellt, ____ o ___ füll' es ___ ganz, ____ o ___ füll' es ___ ganz. ____

Dies Au - gen - zelt, von dei - nem

Glanz al - lein er - hellt, ____ o ___ füll' es ___

ganz, ____ o ___ füll' es ___ ganz. ____

Lachen und Weinen.

Gedicht von Fr. Rückert.

Für eine Singstimme mit Begleitung des Pianoforte

componirt von

FRANZ SCHUBERT.

Op. 59. Nº 4.

La_chen und Wei_nen zu jeg_li_cher Stun_de ruht bei der Lieb' auf so

man_cher_lei Grun_de. Mor_gens lacht' ich vor Lust;_____ und wa_

rum ich nun wei _ ne bei des A_ben_des Schei _ ne,

ist mir selb' nicht be_wusst, ist mir selb' nicht be_wusst.

a tempo

mf

pp

Wei_nen und La_chen zu jeg _ li_cher

Stun _ de ruht bei der Lieb' auf so man _ cher_lei Grun _ de.

A _ bends weint' ich vor Schmerz; _ und wa _ rum du er_
wa _ chen kannst am Mor _ gen mit La _ chen, muss ich dich
fra _ gen, o Herz, muss ich dich fra _ gen, o Herz.

cresc.

pp

Im Abendroth.

Gedicht von Carl Lappe.

Für eine Singstimme mit Begleitung des Pianoforte

componirt von

FRANZ SCHUBERT.

1824.

in mein stil _ les _ Fen _ ster sinkt.

Könnt' ich kla _ gen? könnt' ich za _ gen? ir _ re sein an dir und _ mir?

Nein, ich will im Bu _ sen tra _ gen dei _ nen Himmel schon all _ hier,

und dies Herz, eh' es zu _ sam _ menbricht, trinkt noch Gluth und _ schlürft noch Licht,

trinkt noch Gluth und _ schlürft noch Licht.

Der Einsame.

Gedicht von Carl Lappe.

Für eine Singstimme mit Begleitung des Pianoforte

componirt von

FRANZ SCHUBERT.

Zweite Fassung.

Op. 41.

1825.

so leicht, so un_be_schwert, so leicht, so un_be_schwert. Ein

trau_tes stil_les Stündchen bleibt man noch gern am Feu_er_wach, man schürt,

wann sich die Lo_he senkt, die Fun_ken auf, und sinnt,

und denkt, nun a_ber_mal ein Tag! nun a_ber_mal ein

Tag! Was Lie_bes o_der Lei_des sein

Lauf für uns da _ her ge _ bracht, was Lie _ bes o _ der Lei _ des sein Lauf für uns da _

her ge _ bracht, es geht noch einmal durch den Sinn; al _ lein das Bö _ se _ wirft man hin, _

es stö _ re nicht die Nacht, es stö _ re nicht die Nacht. Zu

ei _ nem frohen Trau _ me be _ rei _ tet _ man ge _ mach sich zu, wann

sor _ ge _ los ein hol _ des Bild mit sanf _ ter Lust die Seele füllt, ergiebt man sich der

Ruh, er giebt man sich der Ruh. O wie ich mir ge-

fal le in mei ner stillen Länd lich keit! Was in dem Schwarm der lau ten Welt das

ir re Herz ge fes selt hält, giebt nicht Zu frieden heit, giebt nicht Zu frieden

heit. Zirpt im mer, lie be Heimchen, in meiner Klause,

eng und klein, zirpt im mer, lie be Heimchen, in meiner Klause, eng und klein,

ich duld'euch gern: ____ ihr stört mich nicht; wann eu _ er Lied das

Schwei _ gen bricht, bin ich nicht ganz al _ lein, bin

ich nicht ganz al _ lein, wann eu _ er Lied das Schwei _ gen bricht,

bin ich nicht ganz al _ lein, bin ich nicht ganz al _

lein, bin ich nicht ganz al _ lein.

Todtengräbers Heimwehe.

Gedicht von Jac.Nic.Craigher.

Für eine Singstimme mit Begleitung des Pianoforte

componirt von

FRANZ SCHUBERT.

April 1825.

Unruhige Bewegung, doch nicht schnell.

Singstimme.

Pianoforte.

O Menschheit, o Le_ben, was

soll's? o was soll's? Grabe aus, scharre zu, Tag und Nacht kei_ne Ruh'!

Das Treiben, das Drängen, wo_hin? o wohin? „In's Grab, in's Grab

tief hin_ab!" O Schick_sal, o trau_ri_ge Pflicht,ich trag's län_ger nicht! Wann

wirst du mir schlagen, o Stun_de_der Ruh'? o Tod, komm' und drü_cke die Augen mir zu,komm' und

drü_cke die Au_gen mir zu! Im

Le_ben, da ist's, ach! so schwül, ach! so schwül, im Gra_be so fried_lich, so

kühl! Doch ach! wer legt mich hin_ein? ich stehe al_lein, so ganz al_

lein, so ganz al_lein! wer legt mich hin_ein? wer legt mich hin_ein?

Langsamer.

Von allen verlassen, dem Tod nur verwandt, ver_weil'ich am Rande, das

Kreuz in der Hand, und star_re mit sehnendem Blick hin_ab_in's tie_fe, in's tie_fe Grab!

Noch langsamer.

Heimath des Friedens, der Se_ligen Land, an dich knüpft die Seele ein magisches Band! du winkst mir von

fer_ne, du e_wi_ges Licht, du winkst mir von fer_ne, du e_wi_ges Licht!

Es schwinden die Ster_ne, das Au_ge schon bricht,

es schwinden die Sterne, das Au_ge schonbricht! Ich sin_ke, ich

sin_ke! ihr Lieben, ich komme, ihr Lieben, ich komm'! Ich sin_ke, ich sin_ke! ihr

Lieben, ich komme, ihr Lieben, ich komm'! ich kom_me, ich komm'!

ich kom_me, ich komm'!

Die junge Nonne.

Gedicht von Jac. Nic. Craigher.

Für eine Singstimme mit Begleitung des Pianoforte

componirt von

FRANZ SCHUBERT.

Op. 43. Nº 1.

1825.

Wie braust durch die Wip_fel der heulende Sturm!

Es klir_ren die Bal_ken, es zit_tert das Haus!

Es rol _ let der Don _ ner, es leuch _ tet der Blitz!

Und fin _ ster die Nacht, und fin _ ster die

Nacht, wie _ das Grab!

Im _ merhin, im _ merhin! So tobt' es auch jüngst noch in

mir! Es brau _ ste das Le _ ben, wie je _ tzo der Sturm! Es

beb _ ten die Glie _ der, wie je _ tzo das Haus! Es flamm _ te die Lie _ be, wie

je _ tzo der Blitz! Und fin _ ster die

Brust,_____ und fin _ ster die Brust,

wie ___ das Grab!

Nun to ___ be, du wil ___ der, ge ___ walt' ___ ger Sturm! ___ Im

Her ___ zen ist Frie ___ de, im Her ___ zen ist Ruh! ___ Des

Bräu ___ tigams har ___ ret die lie ___ bende Braut, ge ___ rei ___ nigt in prü ___ fen ___ der

Gluth, _____ der e _ wi _ gen, e _ _ wi gen Lie _ _ be ge _ traut. Ich har _ re, mein Hei _ land, mit seh _ _ nen _ dem Blick; _ komm, himm _ lischer Bräutigam, ho _ _ _ le die Braut! Er _ lö _ se die See _ le von ir _ discher Haft! Horch! Fried _ lich er _ tö _ net das Glöck _ lein vom Thurm; _____

es lockt mich das sü _ sse Ge _ tön_____ all _ mäch _ tig zu e _ wi _ gen

Höh'n, _____ es lockt mich das sü _ sse Ge _ tön_____ all _ mäch _ tig zu

e _ ___ wi _ gen, e _ ___ wi _ gen Höh'n: Al _ le _

lu _ ___ ja! Al _ le _ lu _

ja!

Nacht und Träume.

Gedicht von Matth. v. Collin.

Für eine Singstimme mit Begleitung des Pianoforte

componirt von

FRANZ SCHUBERT.

Op. 43. № 2.

Singstimme.

Pianoforte.

Sehr langsam.

pp

Heil' — — — — ge Nacht, — — — — du sin_kest

nie — der; nie — der wal_len auch die Träu — — me,

wie dein Mondlicht durch die Räu — me, durch der — Men — schen

stil — le, stil — le Brust. Die be-

lau _ schen sie _ mit _ Lust, die be _ lau _ schen sie _ mit _

Lust, ru _ fen, wenn der Tag erwacht: keh _ _ re

wie _ der, hol _ de Nacht! hol _ _ _ de Träume, keh _ ret

wie _ _ der, hol _ de _ Träu _ me, keh _ ret wie _ _

der!

Ellen's Gesang. III.
Hymne an die Jungfrau.

Aus Walter Scott's „Fräulein vom See".
Deutsch von Ad. Storck.

Für eine Singstimme mit Begleitung des Pianoforte
componirt von

FRANZ SCHUBERT.

Op. 52. No 6.

Der Gräfin Sophie von Weissenwolf gewidmet.

1825.

schla _ fen si _ cher bis zum Mor _ gen, ob Men _ schen noch so grausam sind. O
lä _ chelst, Ro _ sen düf _ te we _ hen in die _ ser dumpfen Fel _ sengruft. O
woll'n uns still dem Schicksal beu _ gen, da uns dein heil'ger Trost an weht; der

Jung _ frau, sieh' der Jungfrau Sor _ gen, o Mut _ ter, hör' ein bit _ tend Kind!
Mut _ ter, hö _ re Kin _ des Fle _ hen, o Jungfrau, ei _ ne Jungfrau ruft!
Jung _ frau wol _ le hold dich nei _ gen, dem Kind, das für _ den Va _ ter fleht!

A _ _ _ ve Ma _ ri _ _ _ _ a!
A _ _ _ ve Ma _ ri _ _ _ _ a!
A _ _ _ ve Ma _ ri _ _ _ _ a!

Auf der Bruck.*

Gedicht von Ernst Schulze.

Für eine Singstimme mit Begleitung des Pianoforte

componirt von

FRANZ SCHUBERT.

Op. 93. № 2.

August 1825.

*) Ausflugsort bei Göttingen.

Dehnt auch der Wald sich tief und dicht, doch muss er end_lich sich er _ schlie _ ssen,

und freundlich wird ein fer _ nes Licht, und freundlich wird ein fer _ nes Licht uns

aus dem dun_keln Tha_le grü _ _ _ ssen.

Wohl könnt' ich ü_ber Berg und Feld auf dei_nem schlanken Rü_cken flie _

gen, und mich am bun_ten Spiel der Welt, an hol_ den Bil_dern mich vergnü_ _

gen. Manch Au_ge lacht mir traulich zu und beut mir Frie_den,Lieb'und

Freude, und den_noch eil'ich oh_ne Ruh', und den_noch eil'ich ohne

Ruh' zu_rück, zu_rück zu meinem Lei_ _de.

Denn

schon drei Ta _ ge war ich fern von ihr, die e _ wig mich ge _ bun _ den, drei

Ta _ ge wa _ ren Sonn' und Stern' und Erd' und Him _ mel mir verschwun _ den.

Von Lust und Lei _ den, die mein Herz bei ihr bald heil _ ten, bald zer _ ris _ sen,

fühlt' ich drei Tage nur den Schmerz, und ach, die Freude musst' ich missen, und

ach, die Freu _ de musst' ich mis _ _ _ sen.

Weit sehn wir über Land und See zur wär _ mern Flur den Vo_gel flie _ _ gen; wie soll_te denn die Lie_be je in ih_rem Pfa_de_ sich be_trü _ _ gen? Drum tra _ be muthig durch die Nacht! Und schwinden auch die dunkeln Bahnen, der Sehn_sucht hel_les Au_ge wacht, der Sehnsucht hel_les

Das Heimweh.

Gedicht von Joh. Lad. Pyrker.

Für eine Singstimme mit Begleitung des Pianoforte

componirt von

FRANZ SCHUBERT.

Zweite Bearbeitung.

In G moll Op. 79. № 1.

Dem Dichter gewidmet.

Gastein, August 1825.

welket die Blume, so welkt er ihr ent_ris_sen da_hin; wie den Al_pen geraubt hin_

welket die Blu_me, so welkt_ er ihr ent_ris_ _ _sen da_hin, ihr ent_ris_ _sen da_

hin. Stets

sieht_ er die trau_li_che Hüt_te, die ihn ge_bar, im hel_len Grün um_duf_ten_der

Mat_ten, stets sieht_ er die trau_li_che Hüt_te, die ihn ge_bar, im hel_len

cresc.

Grün um _ duf _ tender Mat _ ten; sieht das dun _ ke _ le

Föh _ ren ge _ hölz, die ra _ gen _ de Felswand ü _ ber _ ihm, und noch Berg auf Berg in er _

schüt _ tern der Ho _ heit _ auf _ gethürmt und glü _ _ hend im

Ro _ _ _ sen schim _ _ mer des A _ bends, und glü _ _ hend im

Ro _ _ _ sen schim _ mer des A _ bends.

Geschwind.

Ängst_lich horcht er; ihm däucht, er hö_re das Mu_hen der Kü_he vom na_hen Ge_hölz,

und hoch von den Al_pen her_un_ter Glöck_lein klin_gen; ihm

däucht,_____ er hö_____re das Ru_____fen der Hir_

ten,   o _ der ein Lied der Sen _ ne _ rin, die mit um _ schlagen _ der

Stim _ _ me   freu _ dig zum Wieder _ hall auf _ _ jauchzt Me _ lo _ die _ en des

Alplands;   im _ _ mer tönt es ihm nach, _____

im _ _ mer tönt es ihm nach. _____

decresc.   pp

Die Allmacht.

Gedicht von Joh. Lad. Pyrker.

Für eine Singstimme mit Begleitung des Pianoforte

componirt von

FRANZ SCHUBERT.

Op. 79. № 2.

Dem Dichter gewidmet.

Gastein, August 1825.

lieb — li — cher Blu — men glü — hend em Schmelz, im Glanz des ster — ne be sä — eten Him — mels, im

Glanz des ster — ne be sä — — e — ten Him — — mels. Furcht — bar tönt sie im

Don — ner — ge — roll und flammt in des Blitzes schnell hinzuckendem

Flug, doch kün — det das po — chende Herz dir fühl — ba — rer noch Je — ho — vah's

Macht, doch kün — det das Herz dir fühl — ba — rer noch Jeho — vah's Macht, des e — —

Sehnsucht.

Gedicht von J. G. Seidl.

Für eine Singstimme mit Begleitung des Pianoforte

componirt von

FRANZ SCHUBERT.

Op. 105. № 4.

März 1826.

schau' in's rei _ ne Blau hin _ ein. Mir

fehlt etwas, das fühl' ich gut, mir fehlt mein Lieb, _

_ das treu _ e_ Blut: und will ich in die

Ster _ ne seh'n, muss stets das Aug' mir ü _ bergeh'n, muss stets das Aug' mir

ü _ _ ber _ _ geh'n. Mein

Lieb, wo weilst du nur so fern, mein schö_ner Stern, mein Au_genstern?

Du weisst, dich lieb' und

brauch' ich ja, dich lieb' und_ brauch' ich ja,

die Thrä _ _ ne tritt mir_ wie _ der

nah'. Da

quält' ich mich so man_chen Tag, weil mir kein Lied ge_lin_gen mag,__

weil's nim_mer sich er_zwin_gen lässt und

frei hin_säu_selt wie der West, und frei hin_säu_selt wie der

West. Wie

mild mich's wie_der grad' durchglüht!__ Sieh'

nur,— das ist ja schon ein Lied!

Wenn mich mein Loos vom Lieb_chen warf, dann fühl' ich, dass ich

sin_gen darf, dann fühl' ich, dass ich sin _ _ gen darf, dass ich

sin _ gen darf.

Fischerweise.

Von Franz v. Schlechta.

Für eine Singstimme mit Begleitung des Pianoforte
componirt von

FRANZ SCHUBERT.

Zweite Fassung.

Op. 96. № 4.

Der Fürstin Kinsky, geb. Freiin v. Kerpen gewidmet.

Fi _ scher fech _ ten Sor _ gen und Gram und Leid nicht an; er _ löst am frü _ hen
singt zu _ sei _ nem Wer _ ke aus vol _ ler _ fri _ scher Brust, die Ar _ beit giebt ihm

Mor _ gen mit leich _ tem Sinn den Kahn, mit leich _ tem Sinn den Kahn.
Stär _ ke, die Stär _ ke _ Le _ bens _ lust, die Stär _ ke _ Le _ bens _ lust.

Da la_gert rings noch Frie _ de auf
Bald wird ein bunt Ge_wim _ mel in

Wald und Flur und Bach,   er ruft mit sei_nem Lie _ de die gold'_ne Son _ ne
al _ len Tie _ fen laut,   und plätschert durch den Him _ mel, der sich im Was_ser

wach,   er_ ruft mit sei _ nem Lie _ de die gold'_ne Son _ ne
baut,   und plät_schert durch den Him _ mel, der sich im Was_ser

wach.   Da la _ gert rings noch Frie _ de auf Wald und Flur und
baut.   Bald wird ein_ bunt Ge _ wim _ mel in al _ len Tie _ fen

Bach,   er ruft mit_ sei _ nem Lie _ de die gold'_ne Son_ne wach.
laut,   und plät_schert durch den Him _ mel, der sich im Was_ser baut.

144

Doch wer ein Netz will stel _ len, braucht

Au _ gen klar und gut, muss hei _ ter gleich den Wel _ len, und frei sein wie die

Fluth, und frei sein wie die Fluth.

Dort an _ gelt auf der Brü _ cke die Hir _ tin,

schlau _ er Wicht! ent _ sa _ ge dei _ ner Tü_cke, ent _ sa_ge dei _ ner

Tü _ cke, den Fisch be_trügst du nicht. Dort an _ gelt auf der Brü _ cke die

Hir _ tin, schlauer Wicht! ent _ sa _ ge_ dei _ ner Tü _ cke, den

Fisch be_trügst du nicht.

Im Frühling.

Gedicht von Ernst Schulze.

Für eine Singstimme mit Begleitung des Pianoforte

componirt von

FRANZ SCHUBERT.

März 1826.

schö_nen Him_mel blau und hell, und sie im Himmel sah, und sie im_ Himmel sah.

Sieh, wie der bun_te Früh_ling schon aus Knosp'und Blü_the blickt! Nicht

al_le Blü_then sind mir gleich, am lieb_sten pflückt'ich von dem Zweig, von wel_chem sie ge_

pflückt, von welchem sie gepflückt. Denn Al_les ist wie da_mals noch, die

Blu_men, das Ge_fild, die Son_ne scheint nicht min_der hell, nicht min_der freundlich

schwimmt im Quell das blau_e Himmels_bild, das blau_e_ Himmelsbild.

wan_deln nur sich Will' und Wahn, es wech_seln Lust und Streit;

ü_ber flieht der Lie_be Glück, und nur die Lie_be bleibt zurück, die

Es vor_

149

Lieb' und ach, das Leid, und ach, das Leid.

O wär' ich doch ein Vög - lein nur dort an dem Wie - sen -

hang, dann blieb' ich auf den Zwei - gen hier und säng' ein sü - sses Lied von ihr den

gan - zen Som - mer lang, den gan - zen Som - mer lang, ich

säng' von ihr den gan - zen Som - mer lang.

Über Wildemann,

einem Bergstädtchen am Harz.

Gedicht von E. Schulze.

Für eine Singstimme mit Begleitung des Pianoforte

componirt von

FRANZ SCHUBERT.

Erschienen als Op.108. No 1.

März 1826.

man_che Mei_le von Höh' zu Höh', von Höh' zu Höh'.

Und will das Le_ben im

frei_en Thal sich auch schon he_ben zum Son_nen_strahl; ich muss vor_ü_ber mit

wil_dem Sinn und bli_cke lie_ber zum Win_ter hin.

Auf grü_nen Hai_den, auf bun_ten Au'n, müsst'ich mein Lei_den nur

im _ mer schau'n, dass selbst am Stei _ ne das Le _ ben spriesst, und ach, nur Ei _ ne ihr

Herz ver_schliesst, nur Ei _ ne ihr Herz ver _ schliesst.

O Lie _ be, Lie _ be, o

Mai _ en _ hauch! _ du drängst die Trie _ be aus Baum und Strauch! die Vö _ gel sin _ gen auf

grü _ nen Höh'n, die Quel _ len sprin _ gen bei dei _ nem Weh'n, die Quel _ len springen bei

dei _ nem Weh'n! Mich lässt du schweifen im dunk _ len

Wahn durch Win _ des _ pfei _ fen auf rau _ her Bahn. O Frühlingsschimmer, o

Blü _ then _ schein, soll ich denn nim _ mer mich dein er _ freu'n? O Früh _ lings _ schim _ mer, o

Blü _ then _ schein, soll ich denn nim _ mer mich dein er _ freu'n, mich dein er _

freu'n?

Ständchen

aus Shakespeare's: „Cymbelin".
Deutsch von A.W. v. Schlegel.
Für eine Singstimme mit Begleitung des Pianoforte
componirt von

FRANZ SCHUBERT.

Während, Juli 1826.

Singstimme.

Pianoforte.

horch! die Lerch' im Ä _ ther _ blau; und Phö _ bus, neu ___ er _ weckt, ___ tränkt

sei _ ne Ros _ se mit dem Thau, der Blu _ men _ kel _ che deckt, ___ der

Da capo
al Fine.

Gesang

(An Sylvia)

aus Shakespeare's „Die beiden Edelleute von Verona".

Deutsch von E. v. Bauernfeld.

Für eine Singstimme mit Begleitung des Pianoforte

componirt von

FRANZ SCHUBERT.

Op. 106. № 4.

Frau Marie Pachler gewidmet.

Währing, Juli 1826.

Schön   und   zart____   seh' ich   sie
ih___   rem   Aug'____   eilt   A____   mor
Je___   den   Reiz____   be   siegt   sie

nahn,____   auf   Him_mels Gunst und   Spur____ weist,
zu,____   dort   heilt er sei_ne   Blind_heit,
lang,____   den   Er_de kann ge_wäh_ren:

dass   ihr_   Al_les   un___   ter_than,____
und   ver_weilt____   in   sü___   sser_   Ruh',
Krän___   ze_   ihr____   und   Sai___   ten_klang,____

dass   ihr   Al___   les   un___   ter_   than.
und   ver_   weilt   in   sü___   sser   Ruh'.
Krän___   ze   ihr   und   Sai___   ten_   klang!

Der Wanderer an den Mond.

Gedicht von J. G. Seidl.

Für eine Singstimme mit Begleitung des Pianoforte

componirt von

FRANZ SCHUBERT.

Op. 80. № 1.

Joseph Witteczek gewidmet.

1826.

un - be - kannt,

berg - auf, berg - ab, wald - ein, wald - aus,

doch bin ich nir - gend, ach, zu Haus.

Du

a - ber wanderst auf und ab, aus O - stens Wieg' in We - stens Grab,

wallst län - der - ein und län - der - aus, und bist doch, wo du bist, zu Haus!

Der Him_mel, end_los

aus _ gespannt, ist dein ge_lieb_tes Hei_math_land;

o glücklich, wer, wo_hin er geht, doch auf der Hei_math Bo_den steht;

glücklich, wer, wo_hin er_geht, doch auf der Hei_math Bo_den steht, auf der Hei_math

Bo_den steht!

Bei dir allein.

dir al _ lein weht mir die Luft so _ la _ bend, dünkt

mich die __ Flur so grün, __ so mild des Len _ zes

Blüh'n, so bal _ sam _ reich der __ A _ bend, so

kühl der __ Hain, __ bei dir al _ lein, __

so kühl der Hain, bei dir __ al _ lein, bei __

cresc.

164

dir _ al _ lein!

Bei dir al _ lein _____ ver _

liert der Schmerz sein Her _ bes, ge winnt die_ Freud' an_

Lust! Du si_cherst mei _ _ ne Brust des_ an _ ge _ stamm_ten_

Er _ bes; ich fühl' mich mein, bei dir _ al _ lein, bei

dir _ al _ lein, bei dir al _ lein! _____ Ich

fühl' mich mein, bei dir _ lein, bei _ dir al _ lein, bei dir _____

_ al _ lein! _____

Wiegenlied

von J. G. Seidl.

Für eine Singstimme mit Begleitung des Pianoforte

componirt von

FRANZ SCHUBERT.

Op. 105. № 2.

Singstimme

Pianoforte.

Langsam.

pp

con Ped.

Wie sich der Äug_lein kind_li_cher Him_mel, schlum_mer_be_la_stet, läs_sig ver_schliesst!

pp

Wie sich der Äug_lein kind_li_cher Himmel, schlummer_be_la_stet,

läs_sig verschliesst! Schlie___sse sie einst so,

cresc.

lockt dich die Er _ _ _ de: drin _ _ nen ist Him_mel,

au _ _ _ _ ssen ist Lust! drin _ _ nen ist Him_mel,

au _ _ _ _ ssen ist Lust!

Wie dir so schlaf_roth glü _ het die Wan _ ge! Ro_ sen aus E _ den

hauchten sie an. Wie dir so schlafroth glü_het die Wan_ge!

Ro _ sen aus E _ den hauchten sie an:

Ro _ _ sen die

Wan _ gen, Him _ _ mel die _ Au _ gen, hei _ _ te _ rer

Mor _ gen, himm _ _ _ li _ scher Tag, hei _ _ te _ rer

Mor _ gen, himm _ _ _ lischer Tag!

Wie des Ge _ lo _ ckes gol _ di _ ge Wal _ lung

küh_let der Schläfe glü_henden Saum! Wie des Ge_lo_ckes gol_di_ge Wallung

kühlet der Schläfe glü_henden Saum! Schön ist das Gold _ haar,

schö _ ner der Kranz d'rauf: träum' du vom Lor_beer, bis _____ er dir

blüht, träum' du vom Lor_beer, bis _____ er dir blüht.

Lieb_liches Mündchen, En_gel umwehn'n dich,

drinnen die Unschuld, drinnen die Lieb'.

Lieb_liches Mündchen, En_gel umweh'n dich,

drinnen die Un_schuld, drinnen die Lieb'.

Wah _ re sie, Kind _ chen,

cresc.

wah _ re sie treu _ lich: Lip _ _ pen sind Ro_sen, Lip _ _ pen sind

p

pp

Gluth, Lip _ _ pen sind Ro_sen, Lip _ _ pen sind Gluth.

p

pp

Wie dir ein En_gel fal_tet die Händchen,

fal _ te sie einst so: gehst du zur Ruh'!   Wie dir ein En _ gel fal _ tet die Händchen,

fal _ te sie einst so: gehst du zur Ruh'!   Schön sind die Träu _ me,

wenn man ge _ be _ tet: und das Er _ wachen lohn _____ mit dem

Traum,   und das Er _ wa _ chen lohn _____ mit dem Traum.

Das Lied im Grünen.

Von Friedr. Reil.

Für eine Singstimme mit Begleitung des Pianoforte

componirt von

FRANZ SCHUBERT.

Erschienen als Op. 115. № 1.

Juni 1827.

Grü _ nen, da lebt es sich wonnig, da wandeln wir ger _ ne und hef _ ten die Au _ gen da _ hin schon von fer _ ne;

und wie wir so wandeln mit hei _ terer Brust, um _ wal _ let uns im _ mer die kind _ liche Lust, im

Grü _ nen, im Grü _ nen.   Im

decresc.

Grü _ nen, im Grü _ nen, da ruht man so wohl, em _ pfin _ det so Schö _ nes,   und

pp

denket behag _ lich an die _ ses und je _ nes,   und zau _ bert von hinnen, ach, was uns bedrückt,

da strei-chen die Wölkchen so zart uns dahin, so zart uns da-hin, da

hei-tern die Herzen, da klärt sich der Sinn, da hei-tern die Herzen, da klärt sich der Sinn, da

klärt sich der Sinn, im Grü-nen, im Grü-nen.

Im Grü-nen, im Grü-nen, da wur-de manch Plänchen auf

Flü-geln ge-tra-gen, die Zu-kunft der gräm-lichen An-sicht entschla-gen, da

stärkt sich das Au _ ge, da labt sich der Blick, sanft wie _ gen die Wün _ sche sich hin und zurück, im

Grü _ nen, im Grü _ nen.

Im Grü _ nen, im
O ger _ ne im

Grü _ nen, am Mor _ gen, am A _ bend, in trau _ li _ cher Stil _ le,
Grü _ nen bin ich schon als Kna _ be und Jüngling ge _ we _ sen,

ent _ kei _ met manch

_pp_

Liedchen und man _ che I _ dyl _ le, und Hy _ men oft kränzt den po _ e _ ti _ schen Scherz, denn
lernt, und ge _ schrie _ ben, ge _ le _ sen, im Ho _ raz und Pla _ to, dann Wieland und Kant, und

leicht ist die Lockung, em _ pfänglich das Herz im Grü _ nen, im Grü _ nen.
glü _ hendes Herzens mich se _ lig ge _ nannt im Grü _ nen, im Grü _ nen.

Ins Grü _ ne, ins Grü _ ne lasst hei _ ter uns fol _ gen dem freund _ li _ chen Knaben!

Grünt einst uns das Le _ ben nicht für _ der, so ha _ ben wir klüglich die grünen _ de

Zeit nicht versäumt, und wann es gegol _ ten, doch glücklich geträumt im Grü _ nen, im Grü _ nen. Lasst

hei _ ter uns fol _ gen dem freundlichen Kna _ ben, lasst hei _ ter uns fol _ gen dem freundlichen Kna _ ben!

Grünt einst uns das Le _ ben nicht für _ _ der,

so ha _ ben wir klüg_lich die grü_nen_de Zeit nicht versäumt, und wann es ge_gol_ten, doch

glück_lich geträumt, und wann es ge_gol_ten, doch glück_lich geträumt im Grü _ nen, im

Grü _ nen.

Der Kreuzzug.

Gedicht von C. G. v. Leitner.

Für eine Singstimme mit Begleitung des Pianoforte
componirt von

FRANZ SCHUBERT.

November 1827.

Sie steigen an dem Seegestad' das ho‿he Schiff hin‿an; es läuft hinweg auf grünem Pfad, ist bald nur wie ein Schwan. Der Münich steht am Fenster noch, schaut ihnen nach hin‿aus: „Ich bin, wie ihr, ein Pil‿ger doch, und bleib' ich gleich zu Haus. Des Le‿bens Fahrt durch Wel‿len‿trug und heissen Wüsten‿sand, es ist ja auch ein Kreuzes‿zug in das ge‿lob‿te Land, in das ge‿lob‿te Land.

Der Winterabend.

Gedicht von C. G. v. Leitner.

Für eine Singstimme mit Begleitung des Pianoforte

componirt von

FRANZ SCHUBERT.

Januar 1828

schnell nun heran der A_bend graut! Mir ist es recht, sonst

ist mir's zu_ laut. Jetzt a_ber ist's

ru_hig, es häm_mert kein Schmied, kein Klempner, das Volk ver_

lief,_ und_ ist müd. Und

decresc.   pp

selbst, dass nicht rass_le der Wa_gen Lauf, zog De_cken der Schnee durch die

Gas _ _ sen auf, zog De _ cken der Schnee durch die Gas _ _ sen

auf.

Wie

thut mir so wohl___ der se _ li _ ge Frie _ den!

Da

sitz' ich im Dun _ keln, ganz ab _ _ ge_schie _ den, so ganz für mich, so

ganz ___ für mich.
Nur der

Mon _ den _ schein kommt lei _ se, kommt lei _ se zu mir in's Gemach.

Er kennt mich schon und lässt ___ mich schweigen, nimmt

nur sei _ ne Ar _ beit, die Spin _ del, das Gold, und spin _ net stil _ le, ___

webt, und lä _ chelt hold,
und hängt dann sein schim _ merndes

Schlei _ er _ tuch rings _ um an Ge _ räth und Wän _ den aus.

sehr leise

Ist gar ein stil _ ler, ein lie _ ber Be _ such,

macht mir gar _ kei _ ne Un _ ruh im Haus. Will_____ er blei _ ben, so

hat_____ er Ort,_____ freut's ihn nim _ mer, so geht_____ er fort, so

geht_____ er fort. Ich

si _ tze dann stumm im Fen _ ster_ gern, und schau _ e hin _ auf in Ge_

wölk ___ und Stern.   Den _ ke zu_rück, ach

weit, gar ___ weit, in ei _ ne schöne, ver _ schwund' _ ne Zeit.

Denk' an _ Sie, an das Glück der Min_ne,

pp

seuf _ ze still und sin_ne,   und sin_ne,

Die Sterne.

Gedicht von C. G. v. Leitner.

Für eine Singstimme mit Begleitung des Pianoforte

componirt von

FRANZ SCHUBERT.

Op. 96. No 1.

Der Fürstin Kinsky, geb. Freiin von Kerpen gewidmet.

Januar 1828.

Wie bli_tzen die Ster_ne so hell durch die Nacht!____

Bin oft schon da _ rü_ber vom Schlummer er _ wacht.____ Doch

schelt' ich die lich_ten Ge _ bil _ de d'rum nicht, _____ sie

ü _ ben im Stil_len manch' heil_sa_me Pflicht, sie ü _ ben im Stil_len manch' heil_sa_me

Pflicht. _____

Sie wal_len hoch o_ben in En_gel_ge_stalt, _____ sie

leuch-ten dem Pil-ger durch Hei-den und Wald._____ Sie schweben als

Bo-ten der Lie-be um-her,_____ und tra-gen oft

Küs-se weit ü-ber das Meer, und tra-gen oft Küs-se weit ü-ber das Meer._____

Sie

blicken dem Dul_der recht mild in's Ge_sicht,_____ und säumen die

Thränen mit sil_bernem Licht._____ Und wei_sen von Grä_bern gar

ppp

tröst_lich und hold _____ uns hin_ter das Blau_e mit

fp

Fin_gern von Gold, uns hin_ter das Blau_e mit Fin_gern von Gold._____

p *pp*

cresc.

So sei denn ge-
segnet, du strah_li_ge Schaar!_____ Und leuch_te mir lan_ge noch
freundlich und klar!_____ Und wenn ich einst lie_be, seid hold dem Ver_ein,_____
_____ seid hold dem Ver_ein,_____ und eu_er Ge_flimmer lasst Se_gen uns sein, und
eu_er Ge_flimmer lasst Segen uns sein!_____

Auf dem Strom.

Gedicht von L. Rellstab.

Für eine Singstimme mit Begleitung von Waldhorn und Pianoforte

componirt von

FRANZ SCHUBERT.

Erschienen als Op. 119.

März 1828.

Nimm die letz‿ten Ab‿schieds‿küs‿‿se, und die

we‿hen‿den, die‿ Grü‿sse, die ich noch an's U‿fer

sen _ _ de, eh' dein Fuss sich schei _ dend wen _ de!

Schon wird von des Stro _ mes Wo _ gen rasch der Na _ chen

fort _ ge _ zo _ gen, doch den thrä _ nen _ dunk _ len Blick zieht die

Sehn _ sucht stets zu _ rück, _ zieht, _ zieht die Sehn _ sucht stets _ zu _

rück!

p

cresc.

Und so trägt mich denn die

mf

Wel___le fort mit un_er_fleh_ter___ Schnel___le.

Hoff _ nungsleer verhallt die Kla _ ge um das schö_ne Hei _ math_land, wo ich ih _ re, ih _ re_ Lie _ be fand.

Sieh, wie flieht der Strand vor ü _ ber, und wie

drängt es mich hin _ ü _ ber,   zieht mit un _ nenn _ ba _ ren

Ban _ den, an der Hüt _ te dort zu _ lan _ den,   in der

Lau _ be dort zu wei _ len; doch des Stro _ mes

Wel _ len _ ei _ len wei _ ter oh _ ne Rast und Ruh, __

ei _ len oh _ ne Rast und Ruh, füh _ ren

mich dem Welt _ meer zu, füh _ ren mich __ dem Welt _ meer

Au _ ges seh _ nend Schwei _ fen kei _ ne U _ fer mehr er _ grei _ fen,

nun, so schau' ich zu den Ster _ nen auf in je _ nen heil' gen

Fer _ nen!

Ach, bei ih _ rem mil _ den Schei _ ne

nannt' ich sie zu _ erst die _ Mei _ ne;

dort vielleicht, o trö_stend Glück! dort be_gegn' ich ih_rem Blick,___ dort,___

dort be_gegn' ich ih___rem Blick.

Bei der Ster_ne mil_dem

Schei_ne nannt' ich sie zu_erst die Mei_ne; dort viel_leicht, o trö_stend

Glück! dort be - gegn' ich ih - rem Blick, _ dort viel - leicht, o trö - stend

Glück! dort be - gegn' ich ih - rem Blick, dort be - gegn' _ ich

ih - rem _ Blick,

dort be - gegn' ich ih - rem Blick.

Der Hirt auf dem Felsen.

Nach Wilh. Müller's Gedicht „Der Berghirt".
Für eine Singstimme mit Begleitung von Klarinette und Pianoforte
componirt von

FRANZ SCHUBERT.

Für Frau Anna Milder-Hauptmann.
Erschienen als Op. 129.

October 1828.

Wenn auf dem höch_____sten Fels ich____
steh', in's tie - fe Thal her _ nie _ der _ seh', und
sin _ ge, und sin _ ge: fern aus dem
tie ___ fen dun ___ keln Thal schwingt sich empor der Wie _ der _ hall,

der Wiederhall der Klüf_te.

Je wei_ter mei_ne Stim_me dringt, je

hel_ler sie mir wie_der_klingt von un_ten, von un_ten. Mein

Lieb_chen wohnt so weit von mir, drum sehn' ich mich so heiss nach ihr hin_

über, hin-über. Je wei-ter mei-ne Stim-me dringt, je

hel_ler sie mir wie_der_klingt _____ von un_ten, von un_ten.

212

sich empor der Wie_der_hall,

der Wiederhall der Klüf_te.

In tie_ _ _ _ fem Gram_ _ _ _ ver _ zehr'_ _ _ _

214

Der Früh‗ling will kom‗men, der Frühling, mei‗ne Freud', nun mach'‗ ich mich fer‗tig zum

Wandern be‗reit,   nun mach'‗ ich mich

fer_tig zum Wandern be_reit. Der Früh_ling will kommen, o Frühling, meine

Freud', der Früh_ling will kom_men, der Frühling, mei_ne Freud', nun

mach' ich mich fer_tig zum Wan_dern be_reit.

Je wei_ter mei_ne Stimme dringt, je hel_ler sie mir wie_der_klingt, je wei ___

Freud', nun mach' ich mich fer_tig zum Wandern be_reit; der Früh_ling will kommen,

der Frühling, meine Freud', der Früh_ling will kommen, der Frühling, mei_ne

Freud', nun mach' ich mich fer _ tig zum Wan_dern be_reit. Je wei _ _ ter die

Stim _ _ me dringt, je hel _ _ _ ler sie wie_der _ klingt; je

wei_____ter die Stim___me dringt, je hel_____ler sie

wie_der_klingt, je wei_ter mei_ne Stim_me dringt, je hel_ler sie mir wie_der_klingt, je

hel_____ler sie wie_____der_klingt.